CultureShock!
A Survival Guide to Medical Safety

Travel Safe

Dr. Paul E. Zakowich

Marshall Cavendish
Editions

This 2nd edition published in 2009 by:
Marshall Cavendish Corporation
99 White Plains Road
Tarrytown NY 10591-9001
www.marshallcavendish.us

First published as *CultureShock! A Traveller's Medical Guide* in 1995 by Times Editions Pte Ltd, reprinted 1996.
© 2009 Marshall Cavendish International (Asia) Private Limited
All rights reserved

The publisher makes no representation or warranties with respect to the contents of this book, and specifically disclaims any implied warranties or merchantability or fitness for any particular purpose, and shall in no events be liable for any loss of profit or any other commercial damage, including but not limited to special, incidental, consequential, or other damages.

No action should be taken based solely on the contents of this publication. Readers should consult appropriate health professionals on any matter relating to their health and well-being. The information and opinions provided in this publication are believed to be accurate and sound, based on the best judgment available to the author, but readers who fail to consult appropriate health authorities assume the risk of any injuries.

Other Marshall Cavendish Offices:
Marshall Cavendish International (Asia) Pte Ltd. 1 New Industrial Road, Singapore 536196 ■ Marshall Cavendish Ltd. 5th Floor, 32-38 Saffron Hill, London EC1N 8FH, UK ■ Marshall Cavendish International (Thailand) Co Ltd. 253 Asoke, 12th Flr, Sukhumvit 21 Road, Klongtoey Nua, Wattana, Bangkok 10110, Thailand ■ Marshall Cavendish (Malaysia) Sdn Bhd, Times Subang, Lot 46, Subang Hi-Tech Industrial Park, Batu Tiga, 40000 Shah Alam, Selangor Darul Ehsan, Malaysia

Marshall Cavendish is a trademark of Times Publishing Limited

ISBN: 978-0-7614-5682-7

Please contact the publisher for the Library of Congress catalogue number

Printed in Singapore by Times Printers Pte Ltd

Photo Credits:
All colour images and black and white photo on pages vi–vii from Photolibrary.
■ Cover photo: Photolibrary

All illustrations by TRIGG and Razalli Lesut

ABOUT THE SERIES

Culture shock is a state of disorientation that can come over anyone who has been thrust into unknown surroundings, away from one's comfort zone. *CultureShock!* is a series of trusted and reputed guides which has, for decades, been helping expatriates and long-term visitors to cushion the impact of culture shock whenever they move to a new country.

Written by people who have lived in the country and experienced culture shock themselves, the authors share all the information necessary for anyone to cope with these feelings of disorientation more effectively. The guides are written in a style that is easy to read and covers a range of topics that will arm readers with enough advice, hints and tips to make their lives as normal as possible again.

Each book is structured in the same manner. It begins with the first impressions that visitors will have of that city or country. To understand a culture, one must first understand the people—where they came from, who they are, the values and traditions they live by, as well as their customs and etiquette. This is covered in the first half of the book

Then on with the practical aspects—how to settle in with the greatest of ease. Authors walk readers through how to find accommodation, get the utilities and telecommunications up and running, enrol the children in school and keep in the pink of health. But that's not all. Once the essentials are out of the way, venture out and try the food, enjoy more of the culture and travel to other areas. Then be immersed in the language of the country before discovering more about the business side of things.

To round off, snippets of basic information are offered before readers are 'tested' on customs and etiquette of the country. Useful words and phrases, a comprehensive resource guide and list of books for further research are also included for easy reference.

CONTENTS

Being well prepared and taking the necessary medical precautions will ensure you and your loved ones an enjoyable and stress-free holiday.

DEDICATION

*This book is dedicated to my wife Fiona
and our two charming daughters,
Tanya and Amanda.*

With the advent of modern commercial air travel, there has been an explosion in the tourist trade. Increasing numbers of tourists and businesspersons are visiting foreign destinations. They may be exposed to diseases that are not ordinarily found in their home country. Worst yet, many have no idea as to what action to be taken should they fall ill. Problems facing travellers who become suddenly ill include: arranging referrals to regional medical centres of excellence, being evacuated for a serious illness and ultimately being repatriated back home for recuperation. These problems are often compounded by difficulties with language barriers.

In response to the multiple health problems that can occur while travelling abroad, I have written *CultureShock! Travel Safe*.

For those in the travel industry, including travel agents, airline staff and hotel personnel, the sections concerning vaccinations and antimalarial drug prophylaxis are particularly useful. These sections will allow those in the industry to advise their clients accordingly as to what vaccinations are required to enter various countries. Furthermore, advice can be given as to what vaccinations are recommended in consideration of the health risk of a particular region, as well as to what vaccinations are optional or not necessary.

For the business traveller who is always short of time and patience, there is a special section of this book that focuses on 'Stress Management while Travelling'.

The backpacker or world traveller should read carefully the sections concerning international medical assistance. It would be prudent for them to add medical assistance coverage to their health insurance policy before they depart on a long journey. Although their medical bills may be covered, health insurance alone will not arrange for immediate on-the-spot medical solutions that may suddenly arise. Such services can range from providing advice on how to treat minor injuries, arranging for hospital admissions, liaison between the treating doctor and the patient's family, or ultimately a medical evacuation to the nearest centre of expertise.

For the adventurous who enjoy hiking and mountaineering, a special section concerning the dangers of high altitude sickness has been included. The chapter not only provides information relating to its symptoms, treatment and prevention, but also instructive lessons as related through a real life story.

Sun worshipers, sailors, beachcombers and all those making plans for 'fun in the sun' should first read the chapter concerning the harmful effects of excessive sun exposure. Otherwise, their fun holiday may be short-lived.

A section of this book addresses the special needs of those travelling with children, the physically handicapped and the mentally ill. There is also a discussion concerning travelling while pregnant, as well as when not to travell.

Topics that are of importance to all travellers include jet-lag free travel, the treatment and prevention of motion sickness, advice concerning food and water precautions in under-developed countries, first aid and what to do if a medical emergency occurs.

A few travel medical case stories have been included to exemplify the need for health care precautions.

This book is also helpful to those planning to relocate to another country. In addition to information concerning endemic health risk, there is a section that is dedicated to climate adaptation whether relocating to the temperate regions or the tropics.

Finally, I wish to acknowledge the contributions made by Dr Lyndon Laminack, previous senior medical coordinator of SOS International. I would also like to thank Ms. Ann Low for her technical support. Most of all, I would especially like to thank my wife Fiona for her encouragement and assistance in getting the manuscript to Marshall Cavendish in time.

I invite corrections, additional information, arguments or feedback of all kinds.

Dr. Paul E. Zakowich

PREPARING FOR YOUR TRIP

CHAPTER 1

'It is thrifty to prepare today for the wants of tomorrow.'
—Aesop, *The Ant and the Grasshopper*

Get Yourself Checked!

Albert had just retired from the civil service and was planning his long awaited trip to the Orient. He was particular in arranging his lodging, transport and sightseeing itinerary. His financial, home and personal affairs were also carefully settled.

He left the United States with peace of mind and was satisfied that everything had been taken care of. However, two weeks after departure, he suddenly developed weakness of the right side of his body and difficulty talking. He was admitted to a hospital in Bangkok. His treating doctors diagnosed that Albert had suffered a stroke as a result of undetected high blood pressure and diabetes. He was started on treatment and his blood pressure and sugars were brought under control. Unfortunately, there was only minimal improvement of his stroke. Arrangements were therefore made to repatriate him home for rehabilitation therapy. His long awaited vacation was suddenly over.

—An elderly tourist whose 'comprehensive'
travel plans did not include a medical check-up

MEDICAL EXAMINATION BEFORE YOUR TRIP

Albert was a meticulous and careful man. However, in the process of arranging his long awaited trip, he neglected the most important consideration—his health!

Many people are unsure as to when to consult their doctor. This is particularly true regarding preventive medical care or for those living overseas. A comprehensive guideline to Clinical Preventive Services is provided by the U.S. Preventive Services Task Force (USPSTF) on their website. In general, many doctors recommend a basic medical check-up every

two to three years for those 19 to 39 years of age. Thereafter, a routine medical check-up is advisable on an annual basis. The 'after 40' check-up should be comprehensive and include an eye examination (with measurement of intraocular pressure to exclude glaucoma), blood pressure readings and examination of the head, neck, heart, chest, abdomen, peripheral pulses, reflexes and nervous system.

Women should have a pelvic examination, pap smear and a breast examination. Rectal examinations should be done for both males and females to exclude rectal growths or tumours.

Routine blood tests should include a fasting glucose, cholesterol level and a full blood count. A urine specimen for analysis and a stool test for occult blood in the stool should also be done.

For those 50 years or older, most health guidelines recommend colonoscopy screening every five to ten years. This test is imperative for those who have noticed blood in their stool or if stool test screening are found to be positive for occult blood.

An ECG is suggested for those 45 years and older. Depending on cardiovascular risk factors, many doctors will also arrange for an exercise treadmill or imaging test to help exclude coronary artery disease which may not be apparent by physical examination and a resting ECG.

A chest X-ray is optional depending on an individual's past travel and domicile (to exclude tuberculosis), as well as personal habits such as smoking.

How often routine mammograms should be done is controversial and recommendations vary among countries. The United States has the most aggressive guidelines, recommending mammography (with or without clinical breast examination) for women aged 40 and older every 1–2 years. The risk of breast cancer increases with age. Women at high risk for developing breast cancer (such as those with first-degree relatives who had breast cancer or those with breast cancer involving the other breast) benefit from regular breast screening compared to low risk. Your family physician can advise you appropriately.

Recent technological advances have greatly minimised radiation exposure. It has been estimated that the total radiation dose of mammography is roughly equivalent to three months background radiation. This may equate to roughly a one in a million chance of developing breast cancer from a mammography examination, or the chances of developing lung cancer from one cigarette. Consequently, most experts consider the risks of radiation from mammography as negligible.

MEDICAL EXAMINATION AFTER YOUR TRIP

Medical check-ups following short duration travel are usually not necessary. Minor ailments such as traveller's diarrhoea, indigestion and colds can be self-treated with over-the-counter medications, drinking adequate fluids and rest. However, travellers with symptoms such as fever, diarrhoea, persistent cough, weight loss, vomiting, jaundice, urinary disorders, skin disorders or genital infections following travel should seek early medical attention. Consideration should also be given to for a medical check-up following extensive travel through regions with suboptimal sanitation or endemic for certain diseases such as malaria. Please tell your doctor all the places that you have visited during the last 12 months. This will alert your doctor to check for any diseases not normally found in your home country. Early detection is particularly important for virulent diseases such

as Falciparum malaria, where early treatment can be life saving. Furthermore, many diseases do not become apparent immediately but many months (or occasionally years) after returning home. Tuberculosis manifested as a persistent cough is an example of an illness which is often overlooked after returning from an endemic region. Other latent diseases include malaria, amoebic dysentery, viral hepatitis, typhoid and parathyroid fever, sexually transmitted diseases, intestinal parasites, schistosomiasis, filariasis, leishmaniasis, trachoma, trypanosomiasis and typhus. Early detection and treatment of these disorders can prevent long-term complications.

Finally, those with chronic diseases are at greater risk during travel and need to take extra precautions. They should prudently consult their doctor before and following a trip.

Preventive health care is essential for a long and healthy life. Always remember, 'prevention is better than cure'.

INTERNATIONAL CERTIFICATES OF VACCINATION

International certificates of vaccination can be obtained from your doctor or public health institution. They are issued under the authority of the World Health Organisation. These certificates are official documents verifying that proper procedures have been followed to immunise travellers against quarantine diseases such as yellow fever. The certificates are essential in permitting uninterrupted international travel. *They must be complete and accurate in every detail* or you may be detained at international ports of entry.

Certain immunisations are required by various countries. Other immunisations and preventive measures are advisable, depending on the traveller's age, previous immunisation status and the nature and duration of travel. Yellow fever immunisations are given only by designated Yellow Fever Vaccination Centres. Other immunisations may be given by any licensed physician.

The certificate also contains personal health information including general state of health, drug allergies, medications or injections taken regularly, eye prescription and contraindications to vaccinations.

The certificate, if filled out properly, can provide valuable information should you fall ill while in a foreign country. These certificates must be printed in English and French. An additional language may also be used.

The international certificate of vaccination is an individual certificate and not to be used collectively. Separate certificates are needed for children as the information should not be incorporated into the mother's certificate.

IMMUNISATION AND VACCINATIONS

Appropriate immunisation and preventative measures are necessary for healthy travel. The following immunisations for travellers are advisable in addition to routine childhood requirements.

Influenza (flu)

There are two types of influenza vaccine. The 'flu shot' is an inactivated vaccine which is given by a needle, usually in the arm. It is recommended for all persons 50 years of age and older, children age six months to five years of age, pregnant women, and to any adult (or child) that has a chronic illness such as those involving the immune system, kidneys, heart, lungs, or has diabetes. Also, the flu vaccine can be given to anyone who just wants to avoid getting the flu. Vaccination is not advisable for those who are allergic to eggs, and children less than six months of age. Also, people who are ill with fever should delay getting the flu shot until they are better.

The other flu vaccine is given as a nasal spray. Since the vaccine is made with a live, attenuated (weakened) virus, it is only approved for people two to 49 years of age and are in excellent health. In contrast to the flu shot, it is not approved for pregnancy.

Pneumoccoccal

The polysaccharide vaccine is recommended for all persons 65 years and older. In addition, people two years or older who have chronic diseases such as immunity suppression (including no spleen), diabetes, heart disorders, respiratory disorders, or kidney disorders should be vaccinated.

Polio

Travellers who have completed their primary polio vaccinations should receive one additional lifetime booster dose, especially if travelling in polio endemic areas. Polio endemic areas include Africa, South Asia, Southeast Asia, and the Middle East. There are two types of vaccine. One is a live attenuated oral vaccine, which is no longer available in the US, but is still given in many countries. The other is the inactivated polio vaccine administered by injection, which may not be available in some countries. Preferably, the inactivated polio vaccine should be given, because of the rare vaccine-induced illness associated with the oral polio vaccine.

Typhoid Fever

Typhoid vaccination is recommended for those travelling in endemic regions. There are two types of vaccine, one given by mouth (tablets), the other given by injection. The Vi polysaccharide typhoid vaccine is given as a single injection and protection last up to two years. Side effects are minimal, the most frequent of which is soreness at the injection site. The oral vaccine provides a comparable degree of protection against typhoid fever. Three or four capsules are given two days apart. Side effects with the oral vaccine are mild and consist of nausea and abdominal discomfort. Rarely will fever or headache occur. Certain kinds of antibiotics should not be taken within 24 hours of the oral vaccine. Since the oral vaccine is a live, attenuated (weakened) vaccine, it should not be given to those with impaired immune systems, certain types of cancer or HIV/AIDS. The oral vaccine should also not be given to those receiving chemotherapy, steroids or other drugs that can affect the immune system. The oral vaccine should also not be given to children less than six years old. Protection last up to five years.

Ideally, either vaccine should be given at least a couple of weeks before travel. Please take note that neither the injection nor the oral typhoid vaccination is 100 per cent protective. Therefore food and drink precautions are advised.

Tetanus and Diphtheria

Whether travelling or not, everyone should receive a primary series of immunisations against tetanus and diphtheria. The primary immunisation is usually given during childhood, after which a tetanus-diphtheria (Td) booster is recommended every ten years. A single dose of adolescent/adult formulation Td that includes the acellular pertussis vaccine (Tdap) is recommended to replace one Td booster dose for persons 11–64 years of age.

Cholera

Two oral vaccines are available. These vaccines provide only brief and limited protection. Therefore, the Center of Disease Control does not recommend them unless a cholera epidemic is in progress.

Japanese B Encephalitis

Vaccination against Japanese B encephalitis, a mosquito-borne disease that occurs in rural Asia, is advisable for summer travellers who anticipate spending nights in rural rice-growing areas where they will be heavily exposed to mosquitoes. Countries where the disease may be a problem include China, Korea, Taiwan, Thailand, Vietnam, India, Nepal, Sri Lanka and the Philippines. For travellers planning an extensive stay at rural areas of these countries, three injections given about one week apart are recommended. The vaccine is not widely available. Protection may persist for at least two years.

Yellow Fever

Yellow fever vaccinations are recommended for travel to rural areas in the yellow fever endemic zones, which include most of tropical South America and most of Africa between 15 degree N and 15 degree S. Some countries in Africa require a certificate of yellow fever vaccination from all entering travellers. Other countries in Africa, South America and Asia require evidence of vaccination from travellers coming from endemic areas.

The vaccination is given as a single dose of live virus vaccine at registered vaccination centres. After vaccination, these centres will issue a certificate of vaccination. The vaccination and certificate are good for ten years. For information concerning yellow fever vaccination requirements for each country, please consult one of the following:

- Health Information for International Travel by the US Department of Health and Human Services, US Government Printing Office, Washington DC, USA 20402
- Strengthening of Epidemiological and Statistical Services, World Health Organisation, 1211 Geneva 27, Switzerland
- the country's regional embassy or health authority

Malaria

Researchers are currently conducting trials in Africa on a vaccine to prevent malaria. Early results have been promising for infants and children. The vaccine can be safely and effectively administered along with other childhood vaccine. Upon successful conclusion of these trials, a commercial vaccine could be produced that would have a profound impact in limiting the malaria scourge. In the meantime, measures to avoid being bitten by mosquitoes remain paramount. Chemoprophylaxis (medication) is recommended for travel to malaria endemic areas and should be started prior to departure and continued after return. Drug recommendations change depending on emerging malaria parasite resistance. Please consult your doctor or infectious disease control centre prior to departure. Additional information concerning malaria is provided in Chapter Seven.

Hepatitis A

This vaccine is advisable for travellers going to underdeveloped areas where food and water sanitation is poor, particularly outside the usual tourist routes. Inadequately cooked cockles are a frequent source of infection. Vaqta, Avaxim and Havrix are inactivated-virus vaccines available in a two-dose series, given six to 12 months apart. Evidence supports protection for at least ten years, and possibly for life. Injection of immune serum globulin (ISG of GG) pooled from human serum provides passive short-term protection from hepatitis A. ISG is reserved for those going to high-risk areas on very short notice, and children less than two years of age.

Hepatitis B

Hepatitis B may be prevented by immunisation with highly effective and well tolerated vaccines that are now widely available. Pharmaceutical companies who manufacture the hepatitis B vaccines include: 1) Merck Sharp & Dohme and 2) Smith, Kline and Beecham. If you plan a long stay in Asia, Africa or Latin America, it is advisable to be vaccinated against hepatitis B. Adults should have a blood test prior to vaccination to exclude existing natural immunity to the virus, in which case vaccination is not necessary. Prevaccination testing of blood to determine immunity status of people from developed countries is not recommended, since it is not cost effective as the prevalence of the virus in these countries is low. Newborns and children should be vaccinated routinely, and as early as possible.

The immediate benefits of vaccination will be protection from hepatitis B infection, delta infection and their related symptoms, plus long-term potential benefits such as a marked reduction in the risk of liver cancer. Please see Chapter Six on viral hepatitis for additional information.

Meningococcal Diseases

There are two vaccines available, the meningococcal polysaccharide vaccine (MPSV4), and the meningococcal conjugate vaccine (MCV4). In the United States, a dose of MCV4 is recommended for children and adolescents 11 through 18 years of age. Vaccination is also recommended for college freshmen living in dormitories, US military recruits, people with damaged (or removed spleen), and tourists who plan to travel to areas where epidemics are occurring (e.g. sub-Saharan Africa from December through June). Vaccination is required for travellers to Mecca, Saudi Arabia during the Haj. MCV4 is the preferred vaccine for people 11 to 55 years of age, but MPSV4 can be used if MCV4 is not available. MPSV4 should be used when giving it to children one to ten years old and adults over 55, who are at risk. Both vaccines are given as a single subcutaneous injection, and will provide protection up to three years

Dengue Fever and Dengue Haemorrhage Fever

Trials for a vaccine against dengue fever are currently being carried out in Southeast Asia under the direction of the World Health Organisation. At present, however, there is no commercially available vaccine to protect against dengue. Therefore, all measures necessary to keep mosquitoes at bay are paramount.

In addition to vaccinations, prevention against infectious diseases in unhygienic regions includes avoiding raw or inadequately cooked food or drinking beverages that have not been boiled or commercially processed. Care should also be taken to minimise exposure to mosquitoes and insect bites.

The above recommendations for immunisations are meant as general guidelines. It is best to consult your doctor early prior to your trip.

The recommended adult immunisation schedule for the United States, 2009 by the Centers for Disease Control and Prevention is provided in the Appendix.

VACCINATIONS DURING PREGNANCY

Ordinarily, live attenuated-virus vaccines are not given to pregnant women or to those likely to become pregnant within the next three months because of the theoretical risk to the developing foetus. In fact, some live attenuated-virus vaccines such as rubella, measles and mumps are actually contraindicated during pregnancy. Fortunately, there has been no evidence of congenital rubella occurring when the vaccine was inadvertently given to pregnant women. Therefore, inadvertent vaccination is not an indication for aborting the foetus.

Although attenuated virus can be detected in respiratory secretions of people vaccinated with the live virus vaccines measles, mumps and rubella, rarely if ever does transmission occur to others. Therefore, these vaccines can be safely given to children of pregnant women. Whereas attenuated polio virus is shed in the stool by persons recently vaccinated with the live oral polio vaccine, this vaccine can also be safely given to children of pregnant women. Experience to

VACCINATION DURING PREGNANCY

Vaccine/Immunobiologic		Use
Immune globulins, pooled or hyperimmune	Immune globulin or specific globulin preparations	If indicated for pre- or post-exposure use. No known risk to fetus.
Diphtheria-Tetanus	Toxoid	If indicated, such as lack of primary series, or no booster within past ten years. No evidence suggests teratogenicity, but waiting until the second trimester is reasonable to minimise concerns about the possibility of an adverse reaction or obstetric outcome.
Diphtheria-Tetanus-Pertussis	Toxoid- acellular	Not contraindicated but data on safety, immunogenicity and outcomes of pregnancy are not available. ACIP recommends Td when tetanus and diphtheria protection are required but Tdap to add protection against pertussis in some situations. Second or third trimester is preferred.
Hepatitis A	Inactivated virus	Data on safety in pregnancy are not available; the theoretical risk of vaccination should be weighed against the risk of disease. Consider immune globulin rather than vaccine.
Hepatitis B	Recombinant or plasma-derived	Recommended for women at risk of infection.
Influenza	Inactivated whole virus or subunit	All women who are pregnant during the flu season; women at high risk for pulmonary complications. Vaccination may occur in any trimester.
Japanese encephalitis	Inactivated virus	Data on safety in pregnancy are not available; the theoretical risk of vaccination should be weighed against the risk of disease.
Measles	Live attenuated virus	Contraindicated; vaccination of susceptible women should be part of postpartum care.

Vaccine/Immunobiologic		Use
Meningococcal	Conjugated	Data on safety in pregnancy are not available; the theoretical risk of vaccination should be weighed against the risk of disease.
Meningococcal	Polysaccharide	Indications for prophylaxis not altered by pregnancy; vaccine recommended in unusual outbreak situations.
Mumps	Live attenuated virus	Contraindicated; vaccination of susceptible women should be part of postpartum care.
Pneumococcal	Polysaccharide	Indications not altered by pregnancy.
Polio, inactivated	Inactivated virus	Indicated for susceptible pregnant women travelling in endemic areas or in other high-risk situations.
Rabies	Inactivated virus	Indications for prophylaxis not altered by pregnancy; each case considered individually.
Rubella	Live attenuated virus	Contraindicated; vaccination of susceptible women should be part of postpartum care.
Tuberculosis (BCG)	Live, attenuated mycobacterial	Contraindicated.
Typhoid (ViCPS)	Polysaccharide	If indicated for travel to endemic areas.
Typhoid (Ty21a)	Live bacterial	Data on safety in pregnancy are not available.
Varicella	Live attenuated virus	Contraindicated; vaccination of susceptible women should be considered postpartum.
Yellow fever	Live attenuated virus	Indicated if exposure cannot be avoided. Postponement of travel preferable to vaccination, if possible.

The above information has been reprinted with permission of the US Department of Health and Human Services.

date has not revealed any risks of the polio vaccine virus to the foetus.

For pregnant women who absolutely must travel in highly endemic regions, both yellow fever vaccine and the oral polio vaccine may be given. However, if at all possible, it is best to defer vaccination with these live attenuated-virus vaccines until either the second or third trimester. This will help minimise the risk of congenital defects that theoretically can occur during the crucial first trimester of pregnancy.

There is no convincing evidence that vaccines made of inactivated bacteria or virus or toxoids pose any risk to the foetus. Also, passive immunisation with immune globulin can also be safely administered during pregnancy.

MEDICAL ALERT TAG

Certain aspects of your medical history may be vital for appropriate treatment. However, if you become unconscious or incapacitated, obtaining this critical information may be impossible. Fortunately, in response to this problem, medical societies throughout the world have set up 'Medical Alert Associations'. These associations have set up registrars of patients who have medical conditions that require urgent recognition. They also issue and distribute wallet-size information cards, bracelets and neck tags that carry critical details of a patient's medical history. Critical medical information can include:

- allergic or adverse reactions to medications (e.g. penicillin, sulphur drugs, tetanus toxoid and aspirin)
- insulin dependent diabetes
- epilepsy
- cardiac disease and arrhythmias
- uncommon blood types and bleeding disorders (e.g. haemophilia)
- medication dependency (e.g. steroids, anticoagulants)

If you have a medical condition that requires urgent recognition in the event of an accident or emergency, then contact your nearest medical alert association. This extra precaution could be life saving!

PACK A MEDICAL KIT

Prudent travellers usually pack a medical kit. Such a medical kit should include an adequate supply of all currently prescribed medications, plus extras in case of a delay. This is particularly true for medications such as insulin, blood pressure and cardiac drugs where a sudden cessation of treatment can lead to grave consequences.

It is also advisable to check with your doctor as to what vaccinations or medication prophylactics (e.g. malaria) are recommended when travelling to less developed regions.

In addition to a basic supply of bandages, dressing and antiseptic topical solutions, the following items are recommended to have available when travelling.

- Bring along paracetamol or acetaminophen tablets for fever, headaches or muscle aches. Aspirin may also be taken, however some people are allergic to it. Furthermore, children can sometimes have adverse reactions to aspirin, therefore, it is better to give them one of the other abovementioned preparations.

- Take along medication for treatment of diarrhoea. For loose stools or mild diarrhoea, taking charcoal tablets, kaopectate or kaolin may be sufficient. Also, bismuth subsalicylate, taken as Pepto-Bismol liquid 60 ml four times a day, can decrease symptoms. Diphenoxylate (Lomotil) and loperamide (Imodium) are strong anti-diarrhoea drugs that can provide immediate relief. However, they should not be used if you have high fever or blood in your stool. These drugs should also be discontinued if symptoms persist longer than 48 hours. Your medical kit should include several packets of oral hydration salts to avoid dehydration. These packets are reconstituted with water as per directions. Fluid intake should be equal or greater than the amount of body fluid loss by diarrhoea and/ or vomiting.

  Travellers with more severe symptoms (e.g. more than three loose stools within eight hours) may benefit from antibiotic treatment such as trimethoprim-sulphamethoxazole (Bactrim), ciprofloxacin (Ciprobay),

norfloxacin(Lexinor), or doxycycline (Vibramycin). Please note that doxycycline should not be given to women who are pregnant or children under ten years old. However, a doctor should be consulted if symptoms 1) persist more than a few days; 2) are associated with high fever, vomiting or dizziness; 3) diarrhoea is voluminous or 4) if there is blood in the stool.

- Antihistamines and decongestants may be needed to alleviate sinusitis, allergies or simple upper respiratory infections (e.g. flu or cold).
- It is a good idea to have a tube of antibiotic cream or ointment for simple cuts and bruises that can quickly become infected, especially in tropical climates.
- Sunblock creams or lotions, in addition to wearing a wide brimmed hat, are a must if you plan to be exposed to the sun. Also bring along gels to protect against lip chapping. Skin lotions such as Calamine or Caladryl will help alleviate skin irritation or rashes.
- Mosquito repellents containing at least 30 per cent diethyltoluamide (DEET) are needed to keep hungry mosquitoes and insects at bay. DEET can, however, cause severe reactions, particularly with prolonged or excessive

use in children or in higher concentrations. Spraying clothing with permethrin (Permanone) and using permethrin-impregnated mosquito nets also help.

- A daily multivitamin tablet may be advisable if your eating habits become irregular or unbalanced.
- For those are prone to motion sickness, nausea or vertigo, it may be wise to carry a supply of antiemetic medication such as prochloroperazine, dimenhydrinate or promethazine. Antiemetic skin patches (Scopoderm TTS) provide similar therapeutic efficiency. They are usually placed behind the ear before embarking on a journey.

An adequately supplied medical kit will allow effective and early treatment, and prevent minor medical problems from becoming major ones. Obviously, any persistent or progressive malady should be brought to the attention of a local physician. In such cases, it is a good idea to have the name and telephone number of your regular doctor in case he needs to be contacted for additional information.

Vacations are meant to be enjoyable and relaxing, and will be when you are prepared against the unexpected.

HEALTH INSURANCE

In this day and age of exorbitant private medical cost, it is essential to have medical insurance. Travellers should obtain a comprehensive global health care plan. Such a plan should include 24-hours medical assistance for emergency treatment, advice and evacuations, in addition to the standard insurance policy which provides only reimbursement of medical cost.

If you are injured in an accident or developed a sudden illness while on a trip, round-the-clock medical assistance plans can provide emergency service such as arranging for specialist consultations, ambulance transportation, hospital care and, if necessary, evacuation to the nearest medical centre.

Medical assistance plans will also provide non-emergency services such as:

- repatriation home after an illness

- storage of your own blood (autologous blood) for future use
- transportation cost of a relative nominated by you (if you are confined to a hospital longer than one week)
- arrange and cover the cost of transporting essential medicine that is not obtainable locally
- in the case of death, arrange and pay for the cost of post-mortem preparation, funeral formalities and repatriation of the remains of the deceased

Not all medical insurance policies provide for 24-hours medical assistance. Make sure yours does and travel with peace of mind.

Another important consideration when choosing medical insurance relates to pre-existing and related illness. A stroke, for example, may be considered as a related condition for someone being treated for hypertension. Most insurance companies will not compensate for pre-existing or related illness unless it has been specifically written in your policy. A pre-existing illness is one for which you have received prior treatment or that you have been aware of.

Some policies will discontinue coverage as soon as your illness is diagnosed as being chronic, while others may substantially revise your premium upward. If at all possible, please have your policy stipulate that you will continue to be re-insurable at the going rates (indefinitely or for at least several years) following any major illness. For instance,

following a severe heart attack, you may need long-term medical care for complications such as heart failure. It is therefore imperative that you will remain re-insurable at affordable rates.

Other major concerns when choosing medical insurance relate to:

- the amount of actual coverage
- reimbursement for outpatient treatment and day surgery
- deductibles

Medical insurance is normally purchased on a per-year basis. However, many insurance companies issue policies on a per-trip basis to cater to those going on short trips. Such coverage is normally for between eight to 90 days. To make it attractive, reimbursement for the loss of baggage, money or cancellation of flights are included.

This is what you should do when making claims. Inform the insurance company within 28 days with written proof. Keep all bills, receipts, reports as proof. Ask the insurance company for a claim form prior to departure, and keep it with you when travelling. Fill in the claim form immediately after discharge from the hospital or clinic. Do it while it is fresh in your mind. Then send the form to the insurance company soonest possible. For the loss of baggage and personal money, make a police report within 48 hours. Keep your report as evidence.

The cost of your policy can be reduced substantially by having (or increasing) a deductible. Alternatively, additional savings are possible by limiting the geographical scope of your coverage. In particular, your premium may be lowered substantially by excluding high medical cost countries like the USA (which are partially inflated because of litigation cost).

Finally, it is important to determine what is not covered in the policy. Make sure you read the fine print. Exclusions will vary among insurers.

Ordinarily, the following conditions will be excluded from coverage:

- AIDS and all human immunodeficiency virus (HIV) diseases and all sexually transmitted diseases

- childbirth, pregnancy, miscarriage, abortions or infertility treatment or tests
- birth defects, congenital illness or hereditary conditions
- psychiatric treatment (unless specifically covered), drug abuse or alcoholism
- injuries related to resistance to lawful arrest or imprisonment, wars, rebellion, riots, as well as all self-inflicted injuries or suicide
- dental work or treatment, eye examinations or hearing aids (unless specified)
- charges related to routine medical check-ups
- cosmetic or plastic surgery

Government health plans (such as Medicare in the USA) may not cover overseas treatments and hospital care. It is best to check with your national health organisation before leaving on a trip.

Remember, always shop and compare health insurance policies. What you pay for and what you get can vary greatly.

CLIMATE CONCERNS

CHAPTER 2

'Nobody is so constituted as to be able to live
everywhere and anywhere; The influence of climate
upon the bodily functions extends so far.'
—Friedrich Nietzsche, German philosopher

Beware of the Cold

Jerry was cross-country skiing during his mid-term vacation. As he was making a sharp turn on a ledge, he suddenly lost his balance and tumbled down the hill and into a shallow brook. The cold water completely soaked all layers of his clothing. He crawled out of the brook, reattached his skis and began skiing back to the lodge which was a good two miles down the trail. However, after a short distance, Jerry began to shiver and his fingers and toes felt numb. He soon became clumsy and had problems with his balance and coordination. He kept falling backwards and his legs could barely support his weight. Upon arrival at the lodge, his friends found him to be confused, incoherent and his speech slurred. Urgent medical treatment was initiated and arrangements made for evacuation to a nearby medical centre.

—A college student suffering from
hypothermia while skiing in New England

ADAPTING TO COLD CLIMATES

Jerry is suffering from hypothermia and is in imminent danger. His defences against the cold have been broken. His body is losing heat faster than it is able to generate, and unless this situation is reversed, his survival is at stake.

What Actually is Hypothermia?

Hypothermia occurs when the core body temperature falls below 35°C (95°F). However, outdoor temperatures below the freezing point are not necessary to cause hypothermia. Hypothermia can also occur at any ambient temperature that is below normal body temperature, whenever conditions are conducive for losing more heat than our bodies can produce.

How do our bodies become cold? In scientific terms, cold is actually the absence of heat. Our bodies do not become cold but actually lose heat. Heat can be lost by four mechanisms—conduction, convection, evaporation and radiation.

Heat is lost by conduction whenever there is direct contact with a colder object (or colder surrounding medium). If submerged in water, heat from the body is rapidly transferred by conduction to the colder water.

Convection is the means by which most of our body heat is lost. In essence, the body is always surrounded by a thin layer of air particles that have become warm as a result of direct contact with the body (conduction). Convection occurs whenever there is a current that removes this thin layer of heated air particles and replaces them with colder ones. Wind chill factor is an example of the body rapidly losing heat by convection.

Heat is also lost by evaporation. This is the primary means by which the body rids itself of excessive heat through sweating.

Radiation is the last way by which heat is lost. Essentially, the body is like a furnace that radiates heat (or energy) to its surroundings.

What Happens to Our Bodies When It Becomes Cold?

When our body temperature drops below normal, a thermostat-like sensor in our brain quickly turns on the body machinery to generate more heat. The muscles are the most effective body tissue for generating heat. They begin to shiver violently when hypothermia occurs.

Secondly, our circulation begins shunting blood away from the skin and the peripheral areas of our body and redirects the flow to our crucial internal organs. In this way, the skin and outer layers of body fat serve to insulate the rest of the body and to help maintain core body temperature. When these adaptive heat conserving mechanisms fail, hypothermia rapidly sets in.

What are the Symptoms of Hypothermia?

When the body temperature falls below 35°C, the muscles begin to shiver intensely and the skin becomes pale or mottled. As the temperature drops further, the muscles become stiff and victims become dizzy, confused, irrational and sluggish. Shivering may stop, and the victim may not even feel cold. When body temperature drops to less than 26.7°C, unconsciousness occurs. The pupils dilate, breathing becomes shallow, the heart rate slows and the peripheral pulses become faint (or absent). At temperatures below 25°C, deep coma occurs with loss of reflexes and pupil response. Death is imminent and soon the heart begins to fibrillate and then stops.

How Can Hypothermia be Treated?

Mild hypothermia is best treated by removing all wet clothing, and then to be completely covered with multiple blankets to prevent further heat loss. Subsequently, the victim should be moved quickly to a warm environment and not given anything to drink or eat until fully conscious. Contrary to folklore, brandy and other alcohol beverages should not be given. Although alcohol causes a sensation of warmth, it dilates peripheral blood vessels and actually increases heat loss. Victims should be warmed gradually. In the field, hot water bottles or heated stones wrapped in clothing can be used. More severe cases of hypothermia require urgent medical attention and evacuation to the nearest medical centre.

How Can Hypothermia be Prevented?

The best way to prevent hypothermia is to dress appropriately. Wear multiple layers of clothing. Air is a good insulator which becomes heated and then trapped in between the layers of clothing. The final layer of clothing should be a jacket or 'wind breaker', which will reduce the effect of wind chill (or convection heat loss). If the body becomes too warm, layers of clothing can easily be removed as necessary. Wool is an excellent insulator, even when partially wet. Wearing mittens instead of gloves will decrease surface to body ratio and reduce heat loss from fingers and hands. Since a significant amount of heat is lost through the head, wearing a hat, hood or scarf is advisable. Avoid becoming wet since excessive heat loss occurs by both conduction and convection, as in Jerry's case when he fell into the icy cold brook while skiing.

Frostnip, frostbite and other peripheral cold injuries are terms that refer to cold injuries of the peripheral parts of the body.

Frostnip is a mild form of cold injury and the effects are reversible. Parts of the body most often affected include the nose, cheeks, ears, fingers, feet and toes. It is characterised by blanching and numbness of the skin. Treatment consists of simply rewarming the injured body parts.

Frostbite (actual freezing) and immersion foot (non-freezing) result in permanent injuries of the extremities or other peripheral body parts.

Immersion foot (also known as trench foot among soldiers) is the result of repeated and prolong exposure to the cold. Injury occurs in the soft tissue of an extremity such as the muscles, ligaments and nerves. However, there is no damage of the blood vessels, therefore circulation remains intact. As a result of this process, the injured extremity can remain painful and sensitive to cold temperature for years.

Frostbite results from actual freezing of the entire peripheral body part. The blood vessels become clotted and damaged. A few days after the injury, the skin becomes swollen and blisters develop. Subsequently, the overlying skin (or appendages) become necrotic, mummified and eventually sloughed off. Treatment of frostbite consist of immersing the injured extremity into room temperature water and gradually warming the water to a maximum of 40°C. After the frost bitten limb has been warmed, the patient should be placed at rest and the extremity kept elevated to prevent swelling. Gauze pads or cotton balls should be placed in between the digits to prevent maceration. Tetanus toxoid should be administered. Topical, oral or intravenous antibiotics are needed to treat infection which is a frequent complication.

Prevention against frostnip, frostbite and other peripheral cold injuries is best done by keeping covered all exposed areas of the body and staying dry. Clothing and footwear that become wet should be immediately changed. Also, avoid wearing constrictive footwear since they may reduce blood flow to the feet and therefore accelerate chilling. Mittens will conserve heat better than gloves because of reduced surface area. Avoid washing frequently since this results in the loss of protective body oils and dead skin cells which help to insulate against the cold.

Diet Modification

Avoid weight gain induced by inactivity and poor eating habits. Eat sensibly during the holidays. Limit alcohol consumption since alcohol itself has many calories, and it may stimulate appetite and reduce one's resolve to limit food intake. Alcohol and caffeine are mild diuretics, and can contribute to dehydration. It is essential to drink at least four to five glasses of water each day. Winter fatigue can be reduced by eating a diet rich in fruits and vegetables, fish and lean meats, and reducing fats and starch (bread, pasta, potatoes, rice and other starchy vegetables). Since sunlight induced vitamin D formation is reduced during the winter, a diet rich in vitamin D and calcium will help prevent osteoporosis. The elderly may also benefit from a vitamin D and calcium supplement.

Medical Disorders Affected By the Cold

Those with heart or respiratory conditions are at particular risk from the cold. As outdoor temperatures plummet, the heart and circulation are stressed to maintain body core temperature. Adding to this, unaccustomed exertion such as snow shovelling or pushing cars can greatly strained the heart. Therefore, these activities should be avoided for those with heart or respiratory problems and the elderly. It is prudent to do some stretching exercises to warm up slowly before going outside.

Asthmatics are at risk during the winter. The cold air induces constriction of the airways and wheezing in asthmatics, particularly during exercise. On top of this, the increase incidence of viral and bacterial respiratory infections during the winter can further exacerbate this condition. Therefore, extra precautions during physical activities need to be embraced. These include: 1) taking medications regularly as prescribed 2) wearing a scarf over the mouth and nose to help warm air and retain moisture and 3) drink plenty of fluids. Finally, asthmatics should not exercise or engage in strenuous activities during extreme cold weather conditions.

Cold weather is a bane to those with dry skin. Since cold air contains less moisture, skin can become dry, flaky and itchy, a condition commonly referred to as 'winter itch'. Treatment consists of applying cream moisturisers to the skin to help reduce evaporation. Those with very sensitive skin should avoid moisturisers that contain lanolin or perfumes. Baths or showers should be with lukewarm water, and restricted to once a day in order to prevent excessive loss of natural body oil. Avoid excessive cleaning, or the use of strong soaps, cleansers or detergents. Clean the body folds, face, hands and feet, while the trunk and extremities can be simply rinsed with water. Afterward, gently pat dry the skin, and apply a moisturiser. Sensitive skin should be protected from the wind and sun. Premature skin aging, wrinkling and cancer can occur in excessive winter sunlight as well as the summer. For prolong outdoor exposure, a sun block with at least a 15-protection factor is advised.

Seasonal Affected Disorder

Seasonal Affected Disorder ('SAD') is a mysterious form of depression that affects many people during the winter. Also known as 'Winter Blues', it is associated with a lack of sunlight during the dark winter months. Sunlight induces production of seratonin in the brain, a chemical associated with alertness and a general sense of well being. Symptoms of SAD include fatigue, irritability, feeling down and an increase in appetite. Affected people may take naps and tend to sleep more, although the quality of sleep is poor. Treatment and prevention involves exposure to intense indoor light, periodic exercise and a diet rich in Triptophan. Some natural paths recommend 5HTP (5-hydroxytryptophan) nutritional supplements. Depending on the severity, sometimes antidepressant medication is necessary. The disorder usually totally resolves by April or May as sunlight becomes more prevalent.

Flu and Respiratory Infection

Since flu (influenza) epidemics commonly occur during the fall and winter, many doctors recommend vaccination against the flu. Pneumococcal vaccination is also recommended for infants, the elderly and those with medical conditions such as heart disease, respiratory disease, and immunodeficiency disorders. It is best to consult your doctor concerning these vaccines.

Driving and Walking

Driving and walking in snow or icy conditions can be hazardous. Cars need to be winterised with antifreeze, winter tires (and chains) and windshield wipers. Emergency winter equipment and supplies include: snow scraper, rock salt, sand, shovels, blankets, warm clothing, flashlights, booster cables, water container and light dry fruits and snacks. A fully charged cell phone is a necessity in case of an emergency. If possible, avoid driving during blizzards, ice storms, or other inclement weather conditions.

Avoid walking on icy or snowy walkways and roads. Wear boots that have non-skid soles. The elderly are particularly prone to falls in slippery conditions. Hip pads are helpful to prevent a fall resulting in a hip fracture. An ice pick can be attached to the bottom of a cane to give greater stability.

WOW ITS HOT! ADAPTING TO THE TROPICS

Those who plan to live or travel in the tropics must adjust to the physical stress associated with higher temperatures, humidity and intense solar radiation. Usually, it takes several days, and sometimes weeks for acclimatisation to occur. During this time, precautions must be taken for those planning vigorous physical activities, sports, or taking arduous walks. Those with heart or breathing disorders are at particular risk to the harmful effects of excessive heat.

What are the Harmful Effects of Excessive Heat?

Besides feeling hot, tired and irritable, there are at least five disorders resulting from excessive heat:

- The most common and least harmful development is 'heat cramps'. This occurs during or after exercise and often in active individuals in good or excellent physical condition. During exercise, the muscles generate internal heat. There is also simultaneous loss of fluids and salts. The combination of these processes results in contraction of the muscles, followed by muscle spasm and cramps. Heat cramps can occur even when outside temperatures are below body temperature. Sun exposure by itself will not cause heat cramps. Treatment consist simply of moving to a cool environment and hydration with fluids. Heat cramps can be prevented by consuming liberal amounts of fluids before exercise.
- Heat exhaustion (also called heat prostration or collapse) is a common condition related to an inappropriate cardiovascular response to high external temperatures. The onset is sudden and the period of collapse short. It occurs in both sedentary as well as physically fit individuals, but is particularly common in elderly individuals taking 'water pills'. Symptoms preceding collapse include fatigue, anxiety, general weakness, thirst, dizziness, headache,

nausea and vomiting. During the collapse, the blood pressure drops, heart rate is rapid and the skin becomes cold and clammy. Body temperature may be normal or even subnormal. Treatment consists of lying the patient down in a cool place with feet elevated and hydrating with oral fluids.

- Exertion heat injury occurs in individuals exerting themselves (such as runners) in high temperatures and humidity. It is more apt to happen in people who are insufficiently acclimatised, not physically conditioned or inadequately hydrated (before and during exertion).

  In contrast to heat stroke, these individuals sweat normally. Symptoms consist of dizziness, goose flesh, headaches, delirium and sometimes loss of consciousness. Urgent medical treatment is essential and involves placing a person in a cold sheet or surrounded by ice packs to immediately lower the body temperature. Oral and often intravenous fluids are necessary, and the victim should be hospitalised for observation.

- The last heat disorder is heat stroke, which occurs most commonly in the elderly who are unable to dissipate excessive heat through sweating.

  Most individuals suffering from heat stroke have chronic diseases such as heart failure, diabetes, alcoholism or are taking medications that impair sweating (examples of such medicine include antidepressants, tranquillisers, beta-blockers, antihistamines, diuretics or vasodilators). Body temperatures can be very high sometimes exceeding 41.1 °C (106 °F). Symptoms may be sudden and are similar to those of exertion heat injury. Heat stroke is a medical emergency and hospital care is mandatory.

- Finally, those not acclimatised to the tropics commonly develop 'prickly heat rash'. Essentially, the skin pores are unable to sweat sufficiently resulting in irritation, redness and itching. Treatment consists simply of keeping cool, wearing cotton clothing and drying the body carefully after washing (especially areas under skin folds). If necessary, calamine lotion or antihistamine creams may also be applied. Avoid powder as it may block skin pores.

How Can Heat Disorders be Prevented?

Drink extra fluids. The body adjusts to excessive heat in two ways. The first and most important way is by sweating. The body can lose large amounts of heat through the process of evaporation. Therefore, it is important that oral fluid intake is sufficient to compensate for increase sweating in hot environments. In fact, as long as there is an adequate supply of isotonic fluids (water containing solutes such as sodium and potassium), the body can withstand very high temperatures by the process of sweating. As acclimatisation occurs, the body is able to sweat more and with a lower salt content.

The other means by which the body loses heat is by dilation of peripheral blood vessels. Sometimes this can result in swelling of the feet and ankles. However, the swelling is harmless and usually resolves after a couple of weeks.

Don't overdo it! When exercising, take a break or rest if you feel hot, tired, thirsty or have muscle aches. These symptoms are often early warnings that your body may be over heating. Take heed, move to a cool place and have a refreshing drink.

Wear comfortable clothing. Wear clothing that is loose fitting and made of porous fabrics such as cotton. This will allow adequate ventilation, sweating and consequently loss of heat from the body. Never wear synthetic materials such as nylon or polyester. Light-coloured clothing reduces heat by reflecting light. Do not wear black clothing since this colour absorbs all light. A wide-brimmed hat is recommended to reduce exposure to the sun.

Stay in a cool place. During heat waves, get out of the sun and avoid stifling environments. Open the windows and use a fan to promote air circulation. Keep a room air-conditioned or visit an air-conditioned facility if you need to take a break from the heat.

POLLUTION

"Doctor, why am I coughing, sneezing and having watery eyes?" asked an expatriate businessman working in Mexico city.

These complaints are becoming commonplace as air pollution becomes a worldwide modern day plague afflicting our post-industrial society. Air pollution can cause symptoms ranging from mild irritation of the eyes, sneezing and cough, to severe respiratory impairment and even death. People with heart, lung and other chronic diseases are particularly at risk.

What is Air Pollution?

In general, pollution can be defined as any change in the environment which inversely affects the quality of human life.

Air pollution is not a recent phenomenon and has been taking place for centuries. Recently, analysis of deep layers of polar ice has provided evidence of air pollutants released into the atmosphere from smelting of ores during the Romans' time. However, its devastating effects only became apparent during the 19th century industrial revolution. Europe, North America and Japan were the places where environmental deterioration first appeared. However, since the 1950s and 1960s, air pollution has become a worldwide problem and of particular concern in densely populated regions.

Air pollution can be divided into two different types—those sources related to indoor pollution and those related to outdoor pollution.

Indoor Pollution

Indoor pollution is particularly associated with those homes and offices that are well insulated and tightly sealed to preserve heat or keep cool. Among the most common indoor pollutants are cigarette smoke, nitrogen dioxide (from combustion devices such as ovens, water heaters and space heaters), formaldehyde and other volatile organic compounds, asbestos and radon.

Passive cigarette smoke has been associated with a variety of respiratory illnesses as well as lung cancer. Studies indicate that non-smokers married to smokers have about a 25 per cent increased risk of lung cancer compared to those married to non-smokers.

After cigarette smoke, some scientists claim that radon gas is the second leading cause of lung cancer. Radon is a naturally occurring radioactive gas which diffuses out of the ground into homes located above subsurface sources. The radioactive gas then attaches to airborne particles which when inhaled can become lodged within lung tissue. Radon gas can be readily measured by professional agencies and corrective steps can be undertaken to reduce exposure.

Exposure to asbestos can lead to scarring of the lung (described as fibrosis in medical jargon) and cancer of the lung as well as the lung lining (pleura). Common sources of asbestos include deteriorating insulation on heating pipes and boilers.

Formaldehyde and other aldehydes are a main source of pollution in buildings. Since they are very soluble in water, these gases are readily absorbed in the lungs. These gases are emitted from urea-formaldehyde resins which are used in flooring and furniture to bond wood products such as particle board, plywood, and chipboard. They are also emitted from urea-formaldehyde foam which is used to insulate buildings. Other sources include cigarette and tobacco products, fabrics, carpets, paints and disinfectants. Environmental conditions known to concentrate these pollutants include high humidity and temperature. Exposure to these gases can result in eye, nose and throat irritation, as well as cough and wheezing from those suffering from asthma. Prevention is best achieved by: 1) proper design and installation of air vents to allow adequate ventilation 2) not using construction materials, insulation, and fixtures containing these substances and 3) limiting the amount of exposure time.

Finally, infectious agents such as bacteria and virus are another type of indoor pollution. Of this group, Legionnaire's disease has been intensely studied. This disease occurs worldwide and is caused by the infectious agent Legionella pneumophila. This bacteria frequently contaminates cooling towers, air conditioning systems, and humidifiers. Hot water systems and heat exchange units are frequently contaminated due to stagnation, infrequent decontamination, and the presence of sediment or decayed plumbing, all of which contribute to suboptimal levels of chlorine. Disseminators facilitate transmission to humans by generating infectious aerosols. The disease is characterised by two well-described syndromes, pneumonic (lung) illness and Pontiac fever. Pneumonic illness typically begins with malaise, headache, muscle aches and weakness. High fever, chills and a dry cough usually appear 24 hours later. Other symptoms include chest pain, breathing difficulties, nausea, diarrhoea, confusion and occasionally abdominal pain. Antibiotics such as erythromycin are effective in treating this disease. However, it is best to see your personal doctor early if you develop any of the above symptoms.

Outdoor Pollution

The major sources of outdoor pollution include the combustion engine, industrial processes, power plants, forest fires and agricultural waste products. The major pollutants from these sources include carbon monoxide, sulphur dioxide, nitrogen oxides, hydrocarbons, ozone, lead and particulate matter (dust and dirt).

Carbon monoxide binds readily to haemoglobin in red blood cells producing carboxyhemoglobin. When this happens, the red blood cells are unable to deliver oxygen to the tissue and organs of our bodies. At concentrations found in certain large cities, it can cause dizziness, fatigue, headaches, dulling of the senses and slowing of the reflexes. At high levels, carbon monoxide poisoning can cause severe brain damage, coma and death. People at particular risk to the effects of carbon monoxide pollutants include those with heart or lung disease undertaking physical activities.

Sulphur dioxide pollutants come primarily from industrial oil and coal combustion for generating power and electricity. Sulphur dioxide can directly damage the lungs. Those already suffering from bronchitis, asthma and emphysema are particularly sensitive to this pollutant.

Nitrogen oxides, similar to sulphur dioxides, are the products of industrial combustion. They also can cause lung injury, especially in those afflicted with chronic lung diseases. Exposed children have been observed to be prone to influenza and other viral infections. Nitrogen and sulphur oxide emissions are chemically changed in the atmosphere to 'acid rain'. Acid rain has been blamed for much of the forest destruction as well as raising the acidity of lakes in parts of Europe and North America. Under conditions of extreme acidity, fish disappear, the food chain is disrupted and lakes become sterile.

Particulate pollution is a general term but covers all the dust and dirt in the atmosphere. It is thought to be an important cause of respiratory diseases and possibly lung cancer.

Major sources of lead pollution include automobiles and smelter factory emissions. Lead may be absorbed either by inhalation or by ingestion of crops that have 'soaked up' this pollutant. High levels of lead in the body can lead to anaemia as well as bone and brain damage. Children are particularly sensitive to lead intoxication. Children with high levels of lead have been found to have serious learning disabilities.

Air pollution can become progressively worse during an inversion. An inversion is a freak weather condition in which warm air rest like a lid on top of cooler air. The warm air not only traps the cooler air but also its pollutants from dissipating.

What Can Be Done to Minimise the Effects of Air Pollution?

During times when the pollution index level is in the hazardous range, one should stay indoors and avoid outdoor physical activities. This is especially true for people with heart, lung or other chronic illness. For mild irritation and redness of the eyes, eye drops or eye wash can provide relief. There are a number of products on the market and your personal doctor or pharmacist can help you choose one.

Antihistamine or decongestant medication may be taken to relieve upper respiratory symptoms such as nasal congestion and phlegm, sneezing and cough. For those prone to lung congestion, wheezing or asthma, anti-bronchospasm inhalers such as salbutamol (Ventolin) and sometimes steroid inhalers such as Becotide (beclomethasone) may be necessary. However, it is best to consult with your doctor for treatment of these more serious respiratory complications.

Air cleaners are also available. There are essentially two types of air cleaners available to the consumer—those that capture particles by electric attraction and those that capture particles by mechanical filtration.

Among the electronic air cleaners, the simplest are the negative-ion generators that impart an electric charge to particles which are then attached to surfaces of the opposite charge.

Negative-ion generators are effective for control of pollen and 90 per cent effective for clearing tobacco and environmental smoke and particulate matter. Their drawback is the frequent need for cleaning and possible production of ozone.

HEPA (high efficiency particulate air cleaners) are very efficient mechanical filtration devices with a minimum efficiency of 0.3 microns particle size. They have one or more layers of either fibre matting or glass fibre paper. For absorption of gas or odours, they also contain activated charcoal or chemical crystals. They are 99.9 per cent effective for removing pollen, mould spores, animal and hair dander, dust, mite allergens, bacteria, viruses, room dust, tobacco smoke, soot and fumes.

DEALING WITH MEDICAL EMERGENCIES

CHAPTER 3

'Help is only a phone call away.'
—The motto of many medical assistance companies

FIRST AID

All travellers should have a basic knowledge of first aid, since there may be times when professional medical care is not immediately available. This chapter addresses the common medical problems or emergencies that may occur while away from home. Comprehensive coverage of this topic can be obtained from the *Red Cross First Aid Manual*.

Sprains, Strains, Dislocations and Fractures

Sprains and strains are synonymous terms that refer to injury to the muscles, ligaments or tendons in the body. They may occur as a result of blunt trauma to a joint or muscle or the result of a hyperextension injury.

Injured joints quickly become swollen, red and painful. Sprain joints are best treated by placing a towel over the injured joint and immediately applying cold or ice packs to help minimise swelling and inflammation. Do not apply ice directly onto the skin since it may cause frostbite. After 15 to 20 minutes, the ice pack should be removed and the joint can be wrapped with a bandage. A firm (but not constricting) bandage wrap will apply gentle pressure and help prevent swelling and bruising. Ice or cold packs can be reapplied as needed during the next 24 hours to relieve pain and swelling. Avoid walking on injured ankles or knees since this will only compound the injury. Elevation of the injured extremity will also help reduce swelling and inflammation.

Analgesics such as paracetamol, aspirin or ibuprofen can be taken to reduce pain. More serious joint sprains and all fractures should be immobilised by splinting. Splinting can be done with a rolled-up magazine or newspaper or slabs of wood strapped together by cloth or tape. The purpose of splinting is to immobilise a fractured joint and therefore limit further injury to surrounding soft tissue, nerves and blood circulation. Significant sprains and all fractures should always be evaluated by a doctor.

Cuts and Skin Abrasions

All cuts and abrasions should be thoroughly cleaned with soap and water. Foreign particles should be meticulously flushed out with water. Antibiotic cream (or ointment) can then be applied and the wound covered with a clean dressing or bandage. Excessive bleeding from deep wounds can be stopped by applying direct compression to the bleeding site. A doctor should then be consulted. A tetanus booster injection should be given if there has not been a prior booster injection within the past ten years.

Burns

Burns can be graded into first degree (when the skin is red and painful), secondary (when the skin is red, painful and with blisters) and third degree (when there is a full thickness skin injury). With third degree burns, the skin appears to be ashen, grey or waxy. Since the entire skin and its nerve endings has been completely destroyed, third degree burns ironically are painless.

Minor burns should be immersed in cold water for immediate relief of pain. The burn injury should then be gently washed with soap and water and an antibiotic ointment (or silver sulfadiazine) applied to prevent infection. Avoid puncturing any blisters since this may allow bacteria to infect the underlying injured tissue. Draining or weeping burn wounds should be covered with a sterile gauze bandage, and the dressing changed daily.

Extensive or deep burn injuries, and those involving the face, eyes or genitalia should always be treated by a doctor.

CPR and the ABC's

If you are on a tour and one of the group suddenly keels over, immediate resuscitation is life saving. Even if you are not trained in CPR, it is better to do something than nothing until medical help arrives. Ideally, everyone should have a basic knowledge of cardiopulmonary resuscitation (CPR). Sudden collapse can occur as a result of heart disease (e.g. cardiac arrest), choking (unable to breath) or a neurologic disorders (e.g. seizure or 'fits').

A brief summary of CPR is provided here. Recommendations for CPR procedures continue to evolve with time. Everyone is advised to attend a certified CPR course to become proficient, and then update their skills every two years. These courses are arranged in most countries by either the local Red Cross organisation or regional medical associations.

If someone suddenly collapses, first check for unresponsiveness. Tap or shake the victim. Ask the victim "are you OK?". If no response, shout for help or immediately call 911 if a cell phone is available . If there are two people present, one should call 911. Then start CPR. Roll the victim onto his back. If you cannot exclude a neck injury, it is best to roll the victim as a single unit supporting the head and neck. If you are not trained in CPR, then provide 'hands-only CPR', which is giving two chest compression per second, until trained medical assistance arrives. If you are trained in CPR and feel competent, then you can either give a cycle of 30 chest compressions follow by two rescue breaths, or you can give 'hands-only CPR'. If an automatic external defibrillator (AED) is available, give one shock as directed before beginning CPR.

Remember the ABC's: airway, breathing, and circulation.

Open the victim's airway. Use the head-tilt/chin-lift method by putting one hand on the forehead and gently pushing downward, while placing two fingers on the chin and gently pushing upward. Then check to see if the victim is breathing. With the airway open, place your ear over the victim's mouth and nose and listen for breath sounds, and observe the chest for respiration movement. If there is no sign of respiration, open your mouth wide, take in a deep breath, make a seal around the victim's mouth and then give two full breaths (each breath should last one to one and a half seconds). Observe for effective air entry by watching for the chest to rise and fall and listen for escaping air.

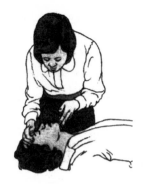

Next, check for a carotid neck pulse. If there is a pulse but no breathing, continue mouth to mouth respiration by giving one breath every five seconds until spontaneous breathing begins or professional medical assistance arrives. If there is no pulse and no breathing, start chest compression as follows: place the heel of your hand on top of the lower half of the victim's breast bone and then lay the other hand over the first. Next, keeping your shoulders squarely over the victim's chest and your elbows locked, compressed the victim's chest at a rate of 120 times per minute. After 30 compressions, give two breaths. Compressions should depress the breastbone by 2 inches (about 5 cm).

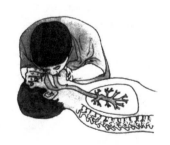

Continue this compression and artificial breathing cycle until the victim's respiration and pulse returns or professional help arrives.

Complications that can occur from excessive forceful chest compression include rib fractures and injuries to internal

organs. Try to prevent your hands from deviating away from the breastbone during compression and onto the abdomen or sides of the chest.

CPR can sometimes be life saving. However, there are situations when it should not be done:

- If the victim is obviously dead.
- If there is evidence of a crush injury of the chest.
- If there is any evidence of spontaneous breathing.
- If the victim has given prior instruction not to be resuscitated as in a 'living will'.

Choking Victims (Who are Conscious)

For choking victims who are still conscious, abdominal thrust should be attempted to help dislodge the obstruction. Abdominal thrusts (also referred to as the Heimllich manoeuvre) are performed as follows:

Stand behind the victim. Wrap your arms around the victim's waist. Make a fist with one hand and place the thumb side of your fist against the middle of the victim's abdomen, just above the navel and *well below the tip of the breastbone*.

Grasp your fist with your other hand. Keeping elbows out, press your fist into the victim's abdomen with a quick upward thrust. Each thrust should be a separate and distinct attempt to dislodge the object. *Repeat thrusts until the airway obstruction is cleared or victim becomes unconscious.*

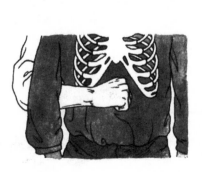

Choking in Infants

- Straddle the baby over your arm with his head lower than his body. Support the baby's head by firmly holding his jaws.
- Deliver four back blows forcefully with the heel of one hand, between the baby's shoulder blades.
- Turn the baby on his back while supporting his head and neck, and place him on your thigh with his head lower than his trunk. Using your index and middle finger, do four chest thrusts at the chest, one finger below the baby's nipple line.

- Check the baby's mouth for any dislodged object. Pick up object with fingers and be careful not to push it further down the airway.
- Repeat the back blows and chest thrusts until the obstruction is removed. If the baby cries, the obstruction would have been removed.

- Bring the baby to the doctor for a check-up.

MEDICAL ASSISTANCE

Business opportunities have taken executives to all corners of the world. At the same time, more holidaymakers are venturing into exotic and remote locations. With this increase in travel, travellers should spare a thought for medical assistance in areas that may not offer the necessary medical services or care at the level to which they are accustomed.

While the traveller can take precautions in the form of a first aid kit, the accessibility of expert medical care is crucial in an emergency. So, who do you contact for a medical problem or even worse a medical emergency? There are several options:

Hotel Doctors

Usually most international or modern hotels have a list of doctors for consultation. Many of these doctors will visit you in your room.

Embassy Referrals

Many embassies have referral lists of English-speaking (or other language) doctors. Some embassies (such as the United States and Canada) actually have their own medical doctors who look after the medical needs of the embassy staff. Although these doctors may be limited to treating only the embassy staff, they can be very helpful in arranging for consultations with local doctors. When calling an embassy for a doctor referral, ask to speak to either the embassy's doctor, nurse or the consular section.

Travel Information Organisations

Before starting your trip, you may obtain an international list of English-speaking doctors from a travel information organisation such as Intermedic or the International Association for Medical Assistance. It is important to realise that such organisations only provide lists of doctors and may not be able to refer you to an appropriate specialist.

International Medical Assistance

For many travellers, an easy solution to their medical needs is to obtain travel insurance or have an agreement with a medical assistance company prior to their trip. Check with your medical insurance company to see if emergency medical assistance is included with your policy. If not, you can buy medical assistance to complement your medical insurance. Medical insurance alone may reimburse your medical expenses, but will not help you to find proper medical attention during an emergency. However, medical assistance companies provide on-the-spot solutions to medically-related problems. Such services include advice on how to treat minor injuries, arranging for hospital admissions, liaison between treating doctor and patient's family or company, and emergency medical evacuation if necessary. Some assistance companies have centres strategically located throughout the world so that the subscriber can easily access their services.

Dr Lyndon Laminack, an American physician who is a senior coordinator doctor of AEA, International, the largest assistance company in the Asia/Pacific area, describes AEA services: "We keep a medical doctor available by phone at all times and the kinds of problems we face vary tremendously. A traveller in Pakistan may require advice for treatment of a minor illness, the wife of a corporate executive in Vietnam may need explanation of malaria prophylactics, or we might be needed to coordinate the evacuation from Bali of an American tourist suffering from head injuries as a result of a car accident". Each year, thousands of cases worldwide are handled by assistance companies like AEA. What assistance services have managed to do is provide the traveller with peace of mind. After all, help is only a phone call away.

BLOOD TRANSFUSIONS

Avoid transfusions, especially from blood banks of less developed countries. If you are involved in an accident which has resulted in excessive blood loss and shock, there may be no other option but an immediate blood transfusion. However, if bleeding has been minimal and there is no danger of circulatory collapse, then it would be prudent to avoid blood products and their associated dangers. Most traumatic haemorrhage can be controlled by direct firm pressure over the bleeding site. For more serious bleeds that require hospitalisation, plasma expander solutions can be given for volume replacement and to maintain blood pressure. In these circumstances, blood transfusion may be delayed until a 'safe source' is available.

What are the dangers associated with blood transfusion?

Allergic Reactions

To begin with, transfusion of other people's blood can sometimes be associated with incompatible adverse reactions such as hives, fever, chills and occasionally shock.

Infectious Disease

Many less developed countries lack the expertise or facilities to adequately screen blood for diseases. Blood can transmit a variety of infectious agents such as viral hepatitis, syphilis, toxoplasmosis, brucellosis, malaria and AIDS. Furthermore, there are many infectious diseases transmitted by blood that cannot be detected even by the most advanced blood banks. Only recently have tests become available that are able to detect for hepatitis C infection.

Transmission of the AIDS virus in developed countries is now rare. However, occasional cases still occur when high risk donors fail to be detected. This is especially true during the early period of virus exposure ('the window period') when antibodies to the virus have not yet developed.

Transmission of Drugs

Blood transfusion can also transfer drugs that result in allergic reactions or cause side effects in certain individuals. People who are allergic to penicillin, aspirin, sulfonamides or other drugs could have a serious allergic reaction when receiving blood containing any of these drugs.

Bacterial Contamination

Blood can become contaminated with bacteria as a result of improper handling and storage. The by-products of bacterial contamination can result in serious side effects such as fever, muscle aches and sometimes septic shock.

Are All Blood Transfusion Unsafe?

The safest blood you can receive is your own. Recently, facilities for storage of autologous blood (one's own blood) have become available for patients planning elective surgery or to have on standby for emergency needs. The blood is frozen at extremely low temperatures (-85°C), and can be stored for up to ten years in accordance with USA Food and Drug Administration standards.

If you are injured away from home, arrangements can be made to transport your own blood to you. Medical assistance companies, themselves, or in cooperation with your insurance policy, often provide this service. Using autologous, blood eliminates all concerns about incompatibility and transmission of infectious diseases.

ANTIBIOTICS AND OTHER MEDICATIONS
Treating infections early and effectively is a concern to all travellers. Antibiotics, introduced in the 1940s, are credited with extending life expectancy by ten years. There are more than 100 different antibiotics available to us to help fight bacterial infections. Here is some useful background information on this family of medications.

They Do Not Cure All Infections
Antibiotics are highly effective in curing bacterial infections, but they're essentially useless in treating viral infections. Even so, some patients with colds or sore throats don't feel their trip to the doctor is complete unless antibiotics are prescribed. Trust your doctor who has been trained to know when an antibiotic is warranted.

Take the Entire Course
When antibiotics are prescribed, take them as directed and take them all. Many people stop taking prescriptions once they start feeling better. Doing this may cause a new, harmful drug-resistant strain of micro-organisms to develop. Because the micro-organism was not completely killed, it bounces back with resistance to that medication. For example, emerging today are deadly strains of tuberculosis resistant to almost every antibiotic and mutant strains of streptococcus are becoming resistant to all traditional antibiotics. The emergence of these virulent resistance strains may not have occurred if people took their medication as prescribed.

Be Aware of How Drugs Mix
Tell your doctor all the drugs you're taking (including over-the-counter medication) because antibiotics can interfere with other medications. For example, erythromycin inhibits liver enzymes production that's needed to metabolise certain other drugs—and two antihistamines, terfenadine (Teldane)

and astemizole (Hismanal) may have serious side effects when taken with erythromycin.

How to Take

Some antibiotics such as tetracyclines are best absorbed when taken before meals (empty stomach), while others should be taken after meals to limit gastric irritation. Your doctor can advise you accordingly.

Pregnancy and Children

Although no antibiotics are known to be completely safe in pregnancy, the penicillin and cephalosporin groups are used most often. Tetracyclines are specifically contraindicated. Furthermore, tetracyclines should *not be* administered to children younger than eight years of age because of adverse effects on developing teeth and bones.

Recognise Side Effects

Adverse side effects sometimes accompany antibiotics. Some of the more common problems are rash, indigestion, abdominal pain, nausea, vomiting and diarrhoea. In women, yeast infections sometimes accompany antibiotics therapy especially in the tropics. Also, certain people may be allergic to groups of antibiotics such as the penicillin. If a side effect occurs, please alert your doctor promptly so that another type of antibiotics can be recommended.

OTHER GROUPS OF MEDICATIONS COMMONLY USED DURING TRAVEL
Aspirin, Ibuprofen, Naproxen and Other Non-steroidal Anti-inflammatory Medications

This group of medications are most commonly taken to relieve pain. In addition, aspirin is also taken to reduce fever. These medications should only be taken as directed and never exceeding recommended dosage. Do not take them on an empty stomach since they can cause nausea and irritation of the stomach lining leading to gastritis, or worse, an ulcer. Many people are allergic to this group of medications, especially those with a history of asthma. If you are one of these people, it is best to consult with your doctor who can prescribe a pain medication that is not part of this group of medications.

Paracetamol and Acetomenophen

These medications are commonly used to relieve pain and fever. They are very safe if taken as directed. Unlike aspirin and related medications, this group will not irritate the stomach and allergic reactions are uncommon. However, exceeding the recommended dosage of these medicines can lead to liver injury.

Antihistamines and Decongestants

These medications are commonly used to relieve the symptoms of colds, flu and upper respiratory infections. They are also used to relieve the symptoms of hay fevers and other respiratory allergies. Antihistamines may cause drowsiness, therefore, it is best to avoid driving or using potentially hazardous equipment while taking them. The newer antihistamines such as terfenadine, astemizole and loretadine do not have this sedating side effect.

Decongestants work by constricting the blood vessels of the mucous membranes, thereby reducing swelling and congestion. However, side effects include rapid heart beat, palpitations, insomnia and raising the blood pressure in some people. Therefore, people with high blood pressure, diabetes or cardiac disease should avoid taking them. Furthermore, they should be taken with caution in those suffering from prostate disease since they may cause difficulty voiding and bladder distension.

TRAVEL RELATED ILLNESSES

CHAPTER 4

'Prevention is better than cure.'
—An old proverb

Struck by Motion Sickness
On the third day of the voyage, the weather took a turn for the worse. The sky turned dark grey and the sea became rough and tumultuous.. The passenger ship tossed from side to side. Joyce felt an unsettling sensation within her stomach. She retired early to her cabin, laid down and tried to read. However, this only made things worse. Suddenly, she lurched forward and with a forceful heave, disgorged her evening's seven-course meal in its entirety.
—A cruise vacationer suffering from sea sickness

PREVENTION AND TREATMENT OF MOTION SICKNESS

Joyce has the typical symptoms of motion sickness. It will probably take another day or two before she gets her 'sea legs'. All of us, at one time or another, have experienced the unpleasant effects of motion sickness. Other names for this malady include sea, air or car sickness, and relate more to the mode of transportation than the process. Even astronauts in space suffer from motion sickness.

What is Motion Sickness?

Motion sickness is a complex topic and is still under intense investigation. Recent research has suggested that some people harbour genes that make them particularly sensitive to this illness.

Certain things are known. Inside our brains is an equilibrium centre that integrates all the sensory information that helps us maintain our balance. Sensory information has three sources—visual (eyesight), somatic (sensors located in our peripheral nerves, muscles and joints) and, most important, the part of the brain called the vestibular system.

The vestibular system includes three small, semicircular canals and two small bones (otoliths) that are located near the eardrums. Normally, information from all three sources work in harmony allowing precise coordination of our movements, be it walking, running or dancing.

Problems occur when there is conflicting information. For example, imagine that you are standing on a rolling ship. Your visual sense sends information to the brain that you are standing still in relationship to your surroundings (the ship). However, the vestibular system sends just the opposite information. That you are actually moving back and forth, up and down, which in fact is the actual relationship of the ship to the ocean. Nerve sensors in your muscles and joints also notice this movement and consequently there is stiffening and tension of muscles and joints. Ultimately, this conflicting array of data greatly disturbs the brain. Confused as to what to do, it sends a message to the stomach to suspend all operations and to eject contents... in a word, vomit.

First, the abdominal muscles tighten. Then there are vigorous convulsions of the stomach, followed by emesis. The medical term for this process is known as 'reverse peristalsis'.

What Can Be Done to Prevent Motion Sickness?
Man has tried to treat this illness since antiquity, when the primary means of travel was by wooden canoes. Many types of plant and food remedies have been used in vain. Although today our knowledge is far from complete, there are proven ways to help alleviate this disorder.

- **Try to Minimise Conflicting Sensory Information**
  This may be done by staying at the centre of a ship or sitting in the wing section of an aeroplane where there is less rocking movements. Another helpful technique is to look at the horizon when in a boat or plane or to

sit in the front seat of a car. These manoeuvres will restore the harmony of the data coming from the visual and vestibular senses.

- **Meals and Psychological Adjustment**
  Eat only small, low-fat starchy meals before and during your trip. Try to relax and rest. Anxiety can stimulate many of the same hormonal reactions that cause nausea. Keep busy with thoughts. In one study, subjects asked to solve mental problems were less likely to develop motion sickness.

- **Adaptation**
  Our brains are able to adjust to motion sickness within a couple of days, for example, seasoned sailors seldom become seasick. The brain adapts simply by ignoring some of the conflicting information.

- **Medications**
  There are a number of medications that will reduce the effects of motion sickness. Most have unpleasant side effects such as drowsiness, muscle spasm, tremor or blurred vision. To be effective, they should be taken before a trip. The three classes of drugs effective against motion sickness are antihistamines (such as dimenhydrinate and promethazine hydrochloride), anticholinergics (such as scopolamine) and the dopamine antagonists (such as metoclopramide).

Scopolamine is easily administered as a skin patch (Transderm Scop). It should be applied behind the ear about four hours before a trip; its effect will last up to 72 hours. Potential side effects include dry mouth, dilated pupils, blurred vision and bladder obstruction in men.

When taking any motion sickness medication, it is advisable to avoid driving or using machinery since the medication can impair concentration. Furthermore, do not take the medication with alcoholic beverages, tranquillisers or other depressant drugs, since they will increase its sedative effects.

- **Other Methods**

Recent research has demonstrated relief of motion sickness by a technique resembling acupuncture without needles. Essentially, a pressure device is applied to areas of the body such as the wrist and then worn during trips.

AIR TRAVEL CONCERNS
Jetlag Free Travel

Be on opposite sides of the globe on the same day! Physically possible with the man-made wonder of the 20th century—the aeroplane. You can leave Tokyo at 12 noon for New York and arrive there at 10:15 am the same day.

However, you do have a price to pay when crossing multiple time zones—a total disorientation of your body rhythms and time sequence. The time differences between the point of embarkation and disembarkation could throw chaos into one's sleeping, walking, eating and working routines and this could take days, even weeks to correct.

Jetlag is also often accompanied by symptoms of fatigue, dizziness, nausea, insomnia, irregular bowel movements, muscular aches and a general feeling of being unwell.

If your next trip involves a large time jump, try following these tips:

- **Psychological Time Adjustment**

Set your watch and time schedule according to that of your destination. Let the expression 'mind over matter' take place and your body rhythms and habits will tend to follow in line with your thoughts. Choose a late departure time when flying west and an early departure time when flying east.

- **Meal and Sleep Adjustments**

  On board the plan, you can begin to adjust sleeping and eating habits according to the schedules of your destination. While most airlines serve meals according to the time schedules of the port of origin, it is left to you to adjust your own meal times correspondingly.

  It may be helpful to take a high protein breakfast and lunch, and high carbohydrate supper to ensure a wakeful day and restful night. Where it is night-time at your destination, wear a sleep mask, earplugs and try to sleep. Correspondingly, when it is daytime, turn on the light above your seat and try to keep awake. Most airlines will show the latest movies on long haul flights to help you while away the travelling hours. This may also be the best time to catch up with all the reading that you have been putting off.

- **Drink Plenty of Water**

  Flying at high altitude, where the air pressure and humidity in the cabin is lower than that on the ground, can leave you dehydrated at the end of the journey. This would make you feel more fatigue and lower your body's resistance to illness. Avoid alcoholic drinks.

- **Follow Local Timetable on Arrival**

  If you arrive in the morning, try to stay outdoors in the sunlight and keep active. Eat light meals during the day and take plenty of fluids, so that you do not overwork your digestive system. If you should arrive at night, take a hot drink (without caffeine) and go straight to bed. By forcing your body to follow these strict rules, you speed up your internal body clock to keep pace with the local timetable.

- **Jetlag Pills**

  Recently, medical research has demonstrated that a hormone called melatonin has a profound effect on the daily rhythm of our internal body clocks. This hormone is secreted by the pineal gland in the brain, and is stimulated by darkness and inhibited by light. There is evidence that

a small dose of melatonin will delay the daily rhythm of the body clock when taken in the morning and advance it when taken in the early afternoon or evening. Many pharmacetical companies have therefore developed pills containing melatonin to help limit the effects of jetlag. Best results are when the melatonin pill is taken 30 to 90 minutes before bedtime on the day of the arrival, then each day of travel thereafter as needed. One study recommended thaking melatonin at 10 pm (destination time) on the same day of flight and for three consecutive days afterwards. Another study recommended taking melatonin between 10 and 12 pm for five days after arrival. There are no known side effects of taking melatonin.

By following the above guidelines, travelling should be easier and will certainly make your trip more enjoyable and comfortable, and help you adjust faster to the new time zone.

Prevention of Blood Clots

For most healthy flyers, the risk of developing blood clots in the deep veins of the legs when flying is small. However, the risk increases significantly for those with a history of: 1) previous deep venous thrombosis (DVT) or pulmonary embolus 2) a close family member who had DVT or pulmonary embolus 3) the use of birth control pills or hormone replacement therapy (HRT) 4) pregnancy 5) cancer 6) recent surgery or trauma, particularly to the abdomen, pelvis or legs 7) those with genetic blood clotting abnormalities. Also known as phlebitis, the risk of developing this condition is strongly correlated to the duration of inactivity while in flight. Symptoms are those of leg swelling, aching and pain. However, sometimes there can be minimal or no symptoms at all. If left untreated, it may result in permanent damage to the circulation of the legs. The most dreaded complication of phlebitis is sudden death. This can occur if a large leg clot dislodges and then flows downstream to the heart (a condition referred to as pulmonary embolism).

Simple preventative measures will suffice to reduce the likelihood of phlebitis. These include frequent walking and leg stretching exercises while on flight, as well as drinking plenty of fluids. Once this illness begins, prompt medical assessment is necessary followed by treatment with blood-thinning drugs (anticoagulants).

Barometric Pressure Changes

When airplanes climb in altitude, all air pockets in the body expand. Usually air will expand to about 25 percent in normal commercial aircraft. Similarly, free air in the body will contract at the same level when the airplane descends. Normally, this does not pose a problem in most healthy flyers. However, those medical conditions that restrict the flow or expansion of air can lead to pain and barometric injury during rapid ascent and descent. Those with sinus congestion or infection can develop pain in the ears and sinus cavities, and should avoid flying until better. If this is not possible, then using a nasal decongestant spray or nose drops before departure and before descending may help alleviate this condition. Yawning, swallowing, chewing or sucking sweets may also help to equilibrate air pressure. Gently blowing air while pinching the nose and keeping the mouth shut may also help. Good dental hygiene is also important, since pain can also develop in cavities in teeth. Expansion of intestinal gas can cause mild and transient discomfort. However, patients who have underwent recent surgery or diagnostic procedures that induce air into the body should consult with their doctors before flying. This is particularly so for certain abdominal operations and for detached retinal repairs. Travellers with colostomies should fit a larger bag to allow for air expansion.

Oxygen Tension

Normally air pressure within the cabin is kept within the range 6,000 to 8,000 feet above sea level. At this level, the amount of oxygen in the air drops slightly, and blood oxygen saturation can be 5 to 10 per cent lower. For most people, this level of hypoxia does not cause a problem. However, this lower oxygen saturation can endanger those with heart conditions, angina, respiratory disorders, significant anemia (hemoglobin less than 8.5 g/dL) or sickle cell disease (not trait). For people with these illnesses, supplemental oxygen during flight needs to be arrange ahead of time. Smoking can aggravate hypoxia, and therefore should be discontinued before air travel, if not permanently.

Cabin Humidity

The higher the altitude, the less moisture there is in the air. This can result in dry eyes, mouth, and nasal passages. Lack of adequate mucous membrane moisture may possibly reduce barriers to fight virus and bacterial infections. Dryness can be relieved by adequate oral hydration, and using saline drops for the eyes and nose. Avoid wearing contact lenses, and use glasses instead. Dry skin can be treated with cream or lotion moisturisers.

Cosmic Radiation

Progressive increases in elevation results in greater background radiation. Commercial aircraft typically cruise at altitudes of 11,000 to 12,000 m (36,00 to 40,000 ft). At this time, there has been no convincing evidence that exposure to cosmic radiation at this level can result in health issues.

Turbulence

Turbulence can lead to motion sickness. Passengers need to return to their seats and to properly secure seat belts to avoid traumatic injuries.

Special Considerations

Air travel should be delayed for at least 12 hours following a deep sea dive, and at least 24 hours following multiple dives. This will prevent the development of the bends that can occur during commercial air travel at high altitudes.

Medical Contraindications to Commercial Air Travel

The following medical disorders preclude flying by commercial air travel, unless cleared by the airline's flight surgeon (or doctor) or accompanied by a medical trained escort:

- **Circulatory disorders**
  - following a heart attack (myocardial infarction)
  - following a stroke (cerebrovascular accident)
  - severe elevation of blood pressure (hypertension), until well controlled by medication
  - moderate to severe heart failure
  - aortic or abdominal aneurysm
- **Lung disorders**
  - rupture or collapse of the lung (pneumothorax)
  - Congenital lung cysts
  - difficulty breathing (vital capacity less than 50 per cent)
- **Eye, ear, nose and throat problems**
  - recent eye surgery
  - acute sinusitis or ear infection (otitis media)
  - jaw wired shut (surgical mandibular fixation)
- **Abdominal and intestinal disorders**
  - less than 10 to 14 days after abdominal surgery
  - acute intestinal diseases (e.g. diverticulitis or ulcerative colitis)
  - esophageal varices
  - acute onset of food poisoning (gastroenteritis)
  - vomiting blood (hematemesis)

- **Psychiatric and neurologic disorders**
  - epilepsy (unless well controlled by medication)
  - previous violent or unpredictable behaviour
  - recent skull fracture
  - brain tumor
- **Blood disorders**
  - anaemia (haemoglobin less than 8.5 g/dl or red blood cell count of less than 3 million/UL in an adult)
  - sickle cell disease (except below 6800 m / 22,500 ft altitude)
  - blood diseases with active bleeding (e.g. haemophilia, leukaemia)
- **Pregnancy**
  Beyond 240 days or with threatened miscarriage
- **Infants less than seven days old**
- **Miscellaneous**
  Need for intravenous fluids or special medical apparatus (unless accompanied with a medical escort).

PSYCHOLOGIC ASPECTS OF TRAVEL AND STRESS MANAGEMENT

Time changes, new surroundings and many hours on the move can exhaust and unravel the most experienced traveller. On top of this, there are frustrations associated with flight delays, loss of personal belongings, irregular meals, jetlag and a multiple of other unforeseen circumstances. Hence, it is easy to see why that to many, travel can be summarised in one word—stress.

What is Stress?

The mind can have a profound effect on the rest of the body. Hormones such as adrenaline are released into our blood stream that are powerful stimulants to our body. Scientists describe this state of heighten awareness as 'the fight or flight response'.

This state of tension is of paramount importance in the evolution of animals where short spurts of adrenaline are needed for survival. However, the effects of unremitting stress can be very harmful for humans.

The short-term effects of stress are transient elevation of blood pressure, increased heart rate, increased sweating, cool extremities, dilated pupils, hyperventilation, dizziness and sometimes headaches. When stress is prolonged, disorders of the stomach (gastritis), intestines (irritable bowel and spastic colon), muscular-skeletal (body aches, stiff back and neck, headaches) and cardiovascular (high blood pressure) may develop. The most serious complications of stress are heart attacks, strokes, hypertension and ulcers.

What Can Be Done to Minimise the Ravages of Stress?

Fortunately, there are many proven ways to reduce stress. The following measures will provide a balanced schedule and help reduce stress when travelling.

Planning

First and most important, it is wise to plan a trip and be prepared for unforeseen circumstances. By planning, you are better able to take things in stride. Formulate and follow a reasonable timetable. Keep a day-to-day agenda. This way, you will not be rushing to conclude all tasks and meetings on the last couple of days. Remember the old adage, 'Rome wasn't built in a day'.

Many business travellers work 14 hours a day, plus dining and evening engagements. No wonder they are stressed out. Allow for adequate sleep at night. If you become tired during the day, take a short nap. Remember your company will only look as good as you do. Take a few hours for sightseeing or a diversion. After all, this can be one of the perks of business travel.

Exercise

Physical exercises and stretching not only keep you in shape but are excellent ways to reduce tension. Warm baths, showers and heating pads help to relieve sore and tense muscles. Many hotels have recreational facilities and spas for their guests. Schedule time for exercise.

Diet
Avoid drinking excessive amounts of caffeine. Reduce your intake of coffee, tea and carbonated soft drinks containing caffeine. Avoid consumption of alcohol, especially on long flights, since it may contribute to jetlag. If you smoke, reduce the number of cigarettes per day, or even better, try to quit.

Medications
Mild sedatives or tranquillisers may occasionally be taken to alleviate jetlag associated with long trips. Their frequent use is strongly discouraged because of their potential addictive tendencies and cognitive side effects.

Flight Schedules
When returning home, choose a flight that suits your body's clock to minimise the effect of jetlag. Choose a late departure when flying west and an early departure when flying east.

AIR RAGE
Stress in conjunction with excessive alcohol consumption can result in this condition. Elevated cabin pressures result in lower oxygen saturation and dehydration. This can magnify the deleterious effects of alcohol and impair cogitation and judgement.

Remember, planning and pacing yourself will help control stress. Otherwise, stress will take control of you!

ACCIDENTS
The major causes of disability or death while travelling or living abroad are not infectious. Accidents and particularly those related to motor vehicles account for the vast majority of serious illness while travelling.

Driving conditions especially in developing countries can be hazardous. Road conditions and vehicles maintenance can be suboptimal, motor vehicle regulations lax and traffic congestion excessive. Night driving may even be more risky since roads are often inadequately lit. Night driving should be avoided since intoxicated drivers may be on the road following social functions. Defensive driving becomes even more essential on foreign roads.

What Can Be Done to Reduce the Risk of Accidents When Travelling?

Always wear seat belts and refrain from drinking alcohol while driving. Rent vehicles from only reputable, quality dealers. Avoid riding motorcycles, scooters or trishaws since they provide little if any protection during accidents. Traffic accidents occurring in areas with limited medical facilities are more likely to be fatal. Head and neck injuries are the most common causes for medical evacuation to regional medical centres of excellence. Other accidents requiring medical evacuations include falls, drowning, electrical mishaps and poisoning.

However, medical evacuation is an option available only to those with medical assistance insurance. You should check with your insurance company or employer as to whether you have this coverage.

FOOD AND DRINK CONCERNS

CHAPTER 5

'Which came first, the intestine or the tapeworm?'
—William Burroughs, American author

Watch What You Eat

John and Janice stared at each other across their dinner table. An extensive array of exotic dishes were set before them, but neither could eat. They both felt feverish, nauseated and had incessant rumbling of their tummies. Worse yet, the urge to have another loose bowel movement seemed imminent.

—A couple suffering from travelller's diarrhoea while touring Mexico

TRAVELLER'S DIARRHOEA

John and Janice have contracted the ubiquitous traveller's diarrhoea (better known as 'Montezuma's Revenge' in Mexico). They have not been discretionary with their diet, and are now suffering the consequences.

Travellers to less developed parts of the world often develop gastrointestinal complaints that mar their vacation or business trip.

Diarrhoea is by far the most common health problem of travellers to developing countries. Of the more than 20 million travellers annually from industrialised to developing countries, approximately one-third will develop diarrhoea. The incidence of traveller's diarrhoea varies markedly by destination.

What Causes Traveller's Diarrhoea?

Virtually all cases of traveller's diarrhoea are caused by infectious agents through ingestion of contaminated food or

water. Especially risky foods include raw vegetables, raw meats and raw seafood. Foods sold by street vendors are a common source of enteropathogens. Overall, the most common etiologic agents are enterotoxigenic E. Coli bacteria, which are responsible for 50 to 75 per cent of episodes. Recently, outbreaks of a virulent strain of E. coli intestinal disease has occurred as a result of inadequately cooked hamburger-type ground beef. Less common causes include: other bacteria such as shigella and vibrio parahemolyticus, viruses such as rotavirus and parasites such as amoeba and giardia.

Symptoms
Symptoms usually begin abruptly and include: urgent diarrhoea, abdominal cramps, nausea and low grade fever. In the great majority of cases, the fluid loss is not voluminous and the symptoms subside within three to five days.

How Can You Treat Traveller's Diarrhoea?
Although fluid loss may not be excessive, it is advisable to drink plenty of fluids. For mild diarrhoea, drinking isotonic

fluids (containing solutes such as sodium and potassium salts) may be the only treatment required.

Bismuth subsalicylate, taken as Pepto-Bismol liquid 60-ml four times a day, can decrease symptoms. However, this medication should be avoided for those individuals who do not tolerate salicylates, are allergic to aspirin, have kidney problems or are taking anti-coagulants, probenecid or methotrexate. Side effects include blackening of the tongue and stool and occasionally nausea, constipation and ringing of the ears.

Diphenoxylate (Lomotil) and loperamide (Imodium) both provide symptomatic relief but should not be used if you have high fever or blood in your stool. These drugs should also be discontinued if symptoms persist longer than 48 hours. Patients with more severe symptoms—more than three loose stools within eight hours—may benefit from antibiotic treatment such as co-trimoxazole, commonly known as Bactrim, ciprofloxacin (Ciprobay) or norfloxacin (Lexinor).

How Can You Prevent Traveller's Diarrhoea?

Prevention is often difficult, but certain recommendations can be made to prevent traveller's diarrhoea as well as all other intestinal infections:

- Avoid eating fruit that you cannot peel.
- Avoid eating raw seafood, meat or vegetables.
- Avoid eating food that is not adequately cooked and served piping hot. According to the US Department of Agriculture (USDA), hamburger meat, for instance, should be cooked so that the internal temperature of the patty is 71 °C. For the consumer, this means the hamburger should be cooked until it is grey/brown throughout and not oozing blood.
- Avoid drinking beverages that are not boiled, packaged or bottled. Also avoid putting ice in beverages. Freezing does not kill many virus or bacteria.
- Ice cream and milk products from unreliable sources are a frequent source of intestinal infections. If in doubt, avoid it. Do not drink milk unless it has been pasteurised or boiled.

Some antibiotics such as doxycycline, co-trimoxazole and norfloxacin have been shown to reduce the incidence of traveller's diarrhoea.

However, because of the calculable risk of adverse reactions of administrating prophylactic antibiotics to several million travellers annually and the generally self-limiting course of traveller's diarrhoea, prophylactic antibiotics are not routinely recommended. It is best to be discerning in selecting beverages and dining establishments while travelling in unsanitary environments.

The above information is meant as a general guideline. You should also consult a doctor, especially if symptoms persist more than a few days or are associated with high fever, vomiting or dizziness, if diarrhoea is voluminous, or if there is blood in your stool.

OTHER INTESTINAL DISEASES
Cholera
Cholera is a severe diarrhoea illness that is caused by the organism named Vibrio cholera. The disease is endemic to the Indian subcontinent and Southern Asia. However, sporadic outbreaks continue to occur throughout the world wherever food and water hygiene practices are inadequate. Most recently an epidemic of cholera occurred in South America. Faecal contamination of seafood (particularly shellfish) and water are the most common means of transmission. The incubation period is short, only 24 to 48 hours. The most important aspect of treatment is rehydration. The body loses large amounts of fluids as a result of vomiting and voluminous watery diarrhoea. Most patients can be rehydrated simply by drinking large quantities of oral hydration solutions. Packets are available in most pharmacies and consist of oral hydration salts that are reconstituted with water as per given instructions. The amount of oral hydration solution consumed should be equal if not greater to the amount of fluid lost from the body.

If oral hydration salts are not available, then rehydration should be attempted by drinking large quantities of other fluids, preferably those that are non-sweetened and contain salts (such as commercially prepared soda, soft drinks and juice). Oral hydration is no substitute for medical care. It should be done while seeking medical attention from a physician or trained health care provider.

Please see the sections on traveller's diarrhoea and vaccination concerning prevention.

Typhoid Fever (Enteric Fever)

Typhoid is a febrile disease caused by a group of organisms from the Salmonella family. Humans are the only source of this infection. The disease is transmitted by faecal contamination of food or drink by a food handler with either typhoid fever or a carrier of the organism. The incubation period varies from as short as three days to as long as two months. Treatment is by antibiotics. Please see the sections traveller's diarrhoea and vaccinations concerning prevention.

Giardiasis

This disease is caused by the protozoan Giardia lamblia and occurs throughout the world wherever sanitation is inadequate. It has been estimated that up to 20 per cent of the population in some developing countries may be infected (most as asymptomatic carriers of the disease).

Even in the United States, giardia is now the most common pathogen for outbreaks of diarrhoea. Faecal contamination of water supplies is the usual mode of transmission. The incubation period ranges from one to three weeks. Giardia propagates and extensively colonises the small intestine resulting in symptoms of malabsorption (frequent loose and watery stools, abdominal cramping, flatulence and nausea).

If left untreated, profound weight loss and generalised disability can sometimes occur. The disease can be treated effectively by metronidazole or similar type medications. Please see the section on traveller's diarrhoea concerning prevention.

Amebiasis

Amebiasis is a disease involving the large intestine caused by the organism Entamoeba histolytica. Similar to giardiasis, it has a worldwide distribution and occurs wherever sanitation is inadequate. In certain underdeveloped countries, it has been estimated that as much as 50 per cent of the inhabitants may harbour the parasite. The majority of those infected are asymptomatic carriers and shed numerous cysts in their stools, which in turn contaminates food and water supplies.

Symptoms consist of intermittent diarrhoea often mixed with blood and mucus. Abdominal colic, flatulence and fever also frequently occurs.

More serious complications of infection include amoebic hepatitis, liver abscess and bowel rupture. Metronidazole is usually effective in treating intestinal disease. However, additional medications may be necessary depending on the severity of the disease.

Please see the section on water and food precautions concerning prevention of this disease.

Food-borne Worm Infections

There are three different types of worms that are transmitted by contaminated food or drink: the round worms (nematodes), the tapeworms (cestodes) and the flukes (trematodes). Although these worm infections occur worldwide, they are endemic in the tropics, particularly in areas where sanitation is poor. Diagnosis usually requires careful examination of the stools by a trained technician.

Round worm infections include pinworms(enterobiasis), whipworms (trichuriasis), and giant round worms (ascariasis). Many infestations cause no symptoms. The most common symptom of pinworms is rectal itching, especially at night. Massive whipworm and ascaris infections may result in abdominal colic, diarrhoea, weight loss, anaemia and growth retardation in children. Prevention is by strictly adhering to food and water precautions as previously described. There are a number of effective anti-round worm medications on the market including abendazole (Zentel), mebendazole (Vermox) and pyrantel pamoate (Combantrin).

Flukes are long living worm parasites that invade and damage body organs and tissue. They are transmitted

by eating raw or inadequately cooked freshwater fish (clonorchiasis and opisthorchiasis), freshwater shellfish and crabs (paragonimiasis) or unwashed vegetables (fascioliasis and fasciolopsiasis). Several flukes such as clonorchiasis, opisthorchiasis and fascioliasis can cause severe liver disease and liver cancer. Praziquantel is the drug of choice for treatment of most fluke infections, except for fascioliasis which requires the use of multiple drugs.

The tapeworms are ribbon-like worms that have no mouth or digestive tract. They live within the intestines where they absorb food through the surface of their bodies. Tapeworms infection can occur from eating raw or inadequately cooked beef (taeniasis or beef tapeworm), raw pork (trichinosis or pork tapeworm), or raw fish (diphyllobothriasis). Most people infected have minimal or no symptoms. Mild abdominal discomfort, nausea, excessive passing of gas, weight loss, excessive hunger may occur. Sometimes the pork tapeworm can invade the muscles, internal organs, and even the brain. When this happens, an intense inflammatory reaction occurs resulting in fever, muscle pains, weakness and an increase number of eosinophile cells in the blood. Treatment of tapeworms is by taking either niclosamide (Yomesan) or praziquantel medication.

Tropical Sprue

Tropical sprue is an intestinal disorder that affects residents and visitors to the tropics. The disorder can also occur months or even years later in travellers who have returned from the tropics. Although the cause of this disorder is unknown, plausible aetiologies include:

- nutritional deficiency
- an infectious organism transmitted by contaminated food or drink
- a toxin that is released in the intestine by micro-organisms

Symptoms of the disease are the result of intestinal malabsorption and include persistent diarrhoea, abdominal distension, weight loss, fatigue and generalised weakness. Victims also develop nutritional deficiencies, particularly iron (resulting in anaemia), vitamin B-12 and folate.

A diagnosis of tropical spruce is determined by finding deficiency in at least two nutrients in a symptomatic individual. Biopsy of the small intestine with an endoscope may provide additional support of the diagnosis.

Treatment of tropical sprue is with vitamin B-12, folate and antibiotics (usually tetracycline or a sulfonamide).

WATER TREATMENT

When travelling in regions where sanitation is inadequate, water may be purified by the following means:

First strain water with a clean cloth to remove floating particles and debris. Water can then be treated by either boiling or by chemical disinfection. At high altitude, water should be boiled for at least several minutes to ensure safety. Water may be chemically disinfected by adding iodine by either using tincture of iodine (2 per cent) or by using tetraglycine hydroperiodide tablets (Globaline, Potable-Agua, Coghlan's, etc.). Tincture of Iodine (2 per cent) is readily obtainable at most pharmacies. The following guidelines are recommended when using it to disinfect water:

- Drops (one drop–0.05ml) of tincture of Iodine 2 per cent to be added to one quart or litre of water.
- Clear water—five drops
  Let stand for 30 minutes before drinking.

- Cloudy or cold water—ten drops
  Let stand for at least 60 minutes, or preferably several hours before drinking.

Tetraglycine hydroperiodide tablets may be obtained at pharmacies and sport shops. Water can also be disinfected by chlorination (halazone tablets). However, its germicidal activity is less reliable than iodine and will vary greatly depending on temperature, pH and organic content of the water. All water disinfective tablets should be added as directed.

CONSTIPATION

Many travellers will experience this unpleasant abdominal discomfort, especially on long distance plane journeys. Bowel movements may become infrequent, incomplete or very hard. Our internal body clocks (referred by scientists as diurnal rhythm) are disrupted when passing through multiple time zones. This not only affects our sleeping patterns, but also most of our daily body habits including regular bowel function. Furthermore, flying at high altitude where air pressure and humidity in the cabin are lower than on the ground can leave one dehydrated at the end of a trip. Therefore, bowel movements not only become less frequent but also hard because of lack of moisture. In addition, a lack of exercise during long trips, suppression of urge during inconvenient moments and inadequate allotment of time to pass motion, all contribute to the development of constipation.

What can be done to alleviate constipation while travelling?

First and foremost, always drink extra fluids while travelling, especially during long air flights. A diet high in fibre content (commonly called roughage) such as fruit, nuts, vegetables and bran may also help. Fibre is the part of food that cannot be digested by the intestinal tract. The fibre passes through the bowel undigested and adds bulk to the stool. Fibre increases the moisture content and bulk of stools, therefore stimulating normal bowel movements

Certain medications can induce constipation including some cough suppressants, aluminium hydroxide antacids, iron supplements, antidepressants and some blood pressure medications.

(referred to as peristalsis in medical jargon). Similar to dietary fibre, bulk-forming agents (such as Metamucil) may be taken. These agents are natural, non-pharmacologic preparations containing either psyllium derivatives or methylcellulose. They come in powder form which are easily mixed with either water or juice.

Finally, if the above measures do not work, medication (commonly referred to as laxatives) may be taken. They work by (a) either stimulating the bowel (b) by osmotic retention of large amounts of water with nonabsorbable salts or carbohydrates or (c) by emollient activities that are surface-active wetting and dispersing agents that soften stools by allowing better penetration of fat and water. These agents are generally safe but should only be used for short periods since they completely disrupt normal bowel function and have potential for abuse. They may be administer orally or per rectum.

The following are a few preparations for adults which are widely available. Please check the literature or with your doctor concerning their indication and dosage for children.

Stimulating laxatives
- Bisacodyl (Dulcolax) may be administered orally or by rectum. The adult oral dosage is two or three 5-mg tablet at bedtime. A 10-mg rectal suppository works much quicker and should induce a bowel movement within 15 to 60 minutes.
- Extracts of cascare or senna when taken orally can produce a bowel movement within six to ten hours. The dosage of cascara is 4 to 12 ml which is generally taken at bedtime. The recommended dosage for extract of senna is one tablet once or twice a day.
- Castol oil, the adult oral dose is 15 to 30 ml daily. However, castor oil is more commonly used for bowel preparation preceding radiological examination of the bowel.

Osmotic laxatives
- Milk of magnesia, 15 to 30 ml to be taken once a day.
- Lactulose syrup, 15 to 30 ml to be taken twice to four times daily.

Emollient laxative
- Docusate sodium, 50 to 200 mg once a day.
- Docusate calcium USP, 240 mg once a day.

Constipation that becomes persistent or is associated with blood in the stool should always be investigated by a doctor, since this can be one of the early symptoms of colon cancer.

FIRST TRAVEL STORY

Joan had been living in Bombay for a year. Her husband was a managing director of an international accounting firm. They were both thrilled at the opportunity of living abroad. As an expatriate, the company generously provided many benefits including housing, children education, maid allowance, a chauffeur and car and a paid annual home leave. During her stay in India, she adapted well to the local food and culture and frequented many of the local restaurants. Life was rosy, or so she thought.

Then, about ten months after her arrival, she mysteriously began losing weight and having frequent loose stools. She went to see several doctors who empirically treated her with various antibiotics and digestive medications. Still, her symptoms persisted. She subsequently went to a specialist clinic near Connaught Street who analysed her stools, and ordered stool cultures, laboratory tests, X-rays of her intestinal tract and even abdominal scans. However, no explanation could be found for her symptoms.

During the six weeks of her illness, she had lost almost 20 pounds. The outline of her skeletal frame became visible, she began losing her hair, and her facial features became withdrawn and coarse. Her friends could not believe the sudden change in her physical appearance.

Desperate, Joan started making plans to leave the subcontinent and return to England for further diagnostic tests. Her husband had concurrently made several enquiries with a physician at the Harly Street Clinic.

Fortunately, the last doctor she consulted in Bombay was a gastroenterologist who did an upper endoscopic examination and biopsy of her upper intestine. The biopsy result demonstrated that she was suffering from a parasitic infection, Giardia lamblia.

After treatment with the drug metronidazole, her symptoms promptly resolved within a couple of days. She then gradually regained her weight and her stamina improved. Joan later learned that the parasite was transmitted by food or water contamination.

Despite her past illness, Joan and her husband elected to extend their working assignment in India. However, they have become particular in their eating habits and choice of restaurants.

What did Joan learn from this unfortunate experience?

First, not to eat or drink anything improperly prepared in an underdeveloped country.

The basic rule is—'if you can't boil it, cook it or peel it, then forget it!'

Eating at local restaurants can be safe if the food has been either properly cooked or boiled. Avoid salads, unpeeled fruit, dairy products and unboiled drinks. Do not put ice into beverages, since freezing does not destroy pathologic bacteria, viruses or parasites. Bottled beverages and processed foods are probably safe, although there have been cases of street-side vendors rebottling soft drinks with contaminated water.

Trying the local food can be an integral part of one's cultural experience. But be particular in your eating habits, otherwise your travel itinerary will be confined to the latrines instead of places of interest.

SECOND TRAVEL STORY

Max, a 23-year-old Australian was on a worldwide backpacking tour. While travelling within Mexico, he visited Mexico City, Alcapulco and Taxco (a small village renowned for its silver work).

Max was young, adventurous and impervious to disease or illness, or so he thought. Wisdom is seldom an attribute of youth.

Max liked Mexican food, and being on a budget, primarily ate at street-side vendors. Whether the food was cooked or boiled, as well as other dietary precautions, were not of any concern to Max. On occasions, he would have self-limiting bouts of diarrhoea and abdominal discomfort, but thought nothing of it. One evening, he developed fever, chills and generalised body aches. He took a couple of paracetamol tablets and subsequently felt considerably better. However, the following day, the fever returned with a vengeance and his bed sheets were drenched with sweat. He consulted a local doctor but since his symptoms were not specific, Max was given treatment for the flu. But the fevers and bone-shattering chills were unrelenting. During the next few days, he lost his appetite and began to lose weight. He took a bus back to Mexico City and upon his arrival, consulted the Australian Embassy. They referred him to an English-speaking internist. On physical examination, the doctor noted tenderness of Max's right upper abdomen over the liver.

Max was sent for preliminary laboratory tests which demonstrated non-specific elevation of his liver enzymes. The doctor recommended admission to a hospital. Fortunately, Max had purchased a medical insurance plan prior to his travels that also carried medical assistance. He called their regional alarm city in Mexico City and had a lengthy discussion with their medical coordinator. The medical coordinator, who was a doctor himself, called Max's treating doctor. After discussion, both doctors agreed that admission to a hospital was indicated for diagnostic tests and treatment. The assistance centre acting on the authority of Max's insurance company back home was very helpful. They made all the arrangements for hospital admission and guaranteed all hospital and doctor fees. In addition, they called Max's treating doctor daily for an updated report on Max's condition and treatment. The assistance centre even called Max's family back in Perth, Australia, to inform them of his condition and progress.

While in the hospital, a scan of Max's liver was done which demonstrated a single, well-defined abscess. More specialised blood tests revealed antibodies positive against Entamoeba histolytica infection. On the basis of clinical assessment, abdominal scans and laboratory tests, Max was diagnosed as suffering from an amoebic liver abscess.

Urgent treatment was indicated since this type of abscess can sometimes rupture and cause generalised abdominal infection (peritonitis), septic shock and sometimes death. A drainage tube was inserted under direct X-ray guidance (fluroscopy) into the abscess cavity, and 200 ml of pus was removed. At the same time, Max was started on strong intravenous antibiotics (metronidazole) which are very effective against deep internal amoebic infections. The results of this treatment were dramatic. Within a couple of days, the fever, chills and upper abdominal discomfort resolved, and Max's appetite returned to normal. After five days, he was well enough to be discharged, but had to continue taking oral antibiotics for another week. Max had review appointments with his treating doctor during that time. The doctor advised Max to have discretion with his dietary habits. He discussed the hazards of eating at street-side vendors unless the food was cooked and served hot, and the beverages were either boiled (e.g. tea or coffee) or commercially packaged. He was told not to put ice into drinks since freezing does not kill pathogenic bacteria, viruses or parasites.

At the end of his outpatient treatment, his treating doctor informed Max's assistance company that he was fit to resume his travels. Max, however, was now a wiser traveller. One illness was enough to convince him of the need to adhere to strict food and drink precautions when travelling in less developed regions. Max was also grateful for the prompt and comprehensive assistance provided to him on behalf of his insurance company. He felt reassured knowing that while away from home, medical assistance when needed, was just a phone call away!

VIRAL HEPATITIS

CHAPTER 6

'Virus is the last predator of men.'
—Robin Cook, dialogue of the movie *Outbreak*

Hit by Hepatitis

Something was not right. Initially, she felt nauseated, feverish and fatigue. Then she completely lost her appetite, her stools became an unusual clay colour and there appeared to be a tinge of yellow of the whites of her eyes. However, it was not until her urine became a dark tea colour and her skin turned as yellow as a canary did she seek urgent medical attention.

—A traveller suffering from viral hepatitis A infection following a six-week tour of South America

WHAT IS HEPATITIS?

In simple terms, hepatitis is an inflammation of the liver. It can be caused by viral (e.g. type A, B, C, D, E, F and several others), bacterial or protozoan infections. Toxic chemicals, drugs and alcohol may also damage the liver, leading to hepatitis. During the past several years, effective vaccines have become commercially available against the most common causes of viral hepatitis, types A and B.

What are the Symptoms?

- No symptoms at all (common)
- Loss of appetite
- Jaundice (yellow skin and eyes)
- Dark urine
- Pale faeces
- Fever, chills, muscle and joint aches which make you think you have the flu

- Nausea and sometimes vomiting
- Pain and swelling at the upper right side of the abdomen (where the liver is)
- Persistent tiredness

WHAT IS HEPATITIS B?

Hepatitis B is one of at least five viral strains of hepatitis that affect the liver. Hepatitis B is one of the most serious strains because of the possibility of severe complications such as massive liver cell death (cirrhosis) and a strong association with liver cancer (hepatoma).

After an individual is exposed to the virus, six weeks to six months may elapse before signs and symptoms appear. Complete recovery may take six months or longer.

What are the Possible Results of a Hepatitis B Infection?

- Most people recover completely from the disease and develop life-long immunity.
- Some people infected with the hepatitis B virus do not form antibodies and the virus remains in their blood. These people then become carriers of the hepatitis B virus and can pass the disease to others. They also run the risk of developing liver cancer or cirrhosis 10 to 20 years later.
- Nearly half the family members of those suffering the acute illness may become infected.
- A high incidence of infected newborns become carriers. Many of these carrier babies will later (in adulthood) die of complications of liver disease due to the hepatitis B virus.
- People who have an acute or chronic hepatitis B infection are at high risk of contracting delta agent infection. Delta agent is a recently discovered virus that also infects the liver. Delta agent replicates and causes disease only in persons who are acutely or chronically infected with the hepatitis B virus. Illness resulting from a combined delta-hepatitis B infection is usually more severe than that caused by hepatitis B alone.

Considering that there are estimated to be more than 300 hepatitis B virus carriers in the world, of whom

170 million are Asians, with 45 million of them in Southeast Asia, the chance of getting hepatitis B cannot be ignore.

How is Hepatitis B Virus Spread?

An infected person has hepatitis B virus in his blood, saliva and semen, and may also have the virus in urine, faeces and other secretions. You can get hepatitis B by:

- Sexual contact with an infected person.
- Being born of an infected mother.
- Accidental contact with an infected person's body fluids or secretions through skin cuts, bruises or mucosal membranes of the eyes and mouth.
- Using unsterilised instruments contaminated by an infected person, such as in injections, ear piercing, acupuncture, tattooing or dental procedures.
- Less common modes of contagion include sharing personal items with an infected person which may break the skin, such as a toothbrush, razor, comb or nail clipper.

There is usually no symptoms associated with infection in infancy, but a high incidence of infected babies become carriers for life.

WHAT IS HEPATITIS A?

Unlike hepatitis B, the hepatitis A virus is contracted primarily by food and water contamination. Inadequately cooked cockles are a frequent source of infection. Hepatitis A is endemic in Asia, Africa, the Middle East, Central and South America. Symptoms of the disease are similar to hepatitis B, however, long-term complications such as cirrhosis and liver cancer do not occur.

PREVENTION OF VIRAL HEPATITIS

The hepatitis B virus can be destroyed by treating the personal utensils of carriers with either boiling water or a household bleach such as Clorox.

Hepatitis B may be prevented by immunisation with the highly effective and well-tolerated vaccines that are now available. If you planning a long stay or trip to an endemic region, it is advisable to be vaccinated against hepatitis B. Adults should have a blood test before vaccination to ensure no previous exposure to the hepatitis B virus. If you have been exposed, vaccination is not necessary since you may have already developed your own immunity to this infection. Newborns and children should be vaccinated as early as possible.

The immediate benefits of vaccination will be protection from hepatitis B infection, delta infection, plus long-term potential benefits such as a marked reduction in the risk of liver cancer. Primary vaccination consists of three intramuscular injections that are given in the shoulder or deltoid muscle. After the initial injection, the other two are given at one and then six months later. Both the plasma-derived (no longer produced) and the yeast-derived American and French vaccines have been shown to be effective and generally well tolerated. Side effects are minimal and may consist of local soreness at the site of injection, rashes, tiredness and occasionally fever. They rarely occur and usually subside within a few days.

Basic prevention against hepatitis A infection is by strictly following food and drink precautions as discussed in the section on prevention of traveller's diarrhoea. An effective vaccine against hepatitis A is now commercially available. In the past, partial and short-lasting protection against hepatitis A was provided by immuneglobulin injections—a human plasma-derived product. The new vaccine is manufactured by having the virus grown on human diploid cells. The virus is then extracted and inactivated by formalin, which also inactivates all other viral or infectious agents.

The vaccine is safe and approved by the World Health Organisation. Two intramuscular injections given two to four weeks apart will provide protection for at least one year. A third booster injection is recommended six months later which will extend immunity against hepatitis A for up to ten years. The vaccine is well tolerated and side effects are few

In addition to the standard advice concerning food and water enteric precautions, avoid eating mollusc such as clams and mussels. That is, unless you are absolutely convinced that they are thoroughly cooked.

Before embarking on your journey, visit your doctor for a medical examination and ensure that you have taken the necessary vaccinations, depending on your destination.

The Huangshan Mountain in Anhui province of China offers spectacular views. When organising a trip to mountainous regions, be careful of altitude sickness and plan a gradual ascent.

A concerned city worker wears a face mask to prevent the spread of airborne diseases and also as a protection against pollution.

Help is not far away. (Left) The Austrian emergency car of the Red Cross; (Right) A first aid sign at the Frankfurt International Airport indicating an automatic external defibrillator to be used in the event of a heart attack.

Water features add beauty and calm to the surroundings in resorts and homes. However they can also serve as potential breeding ground for mosquitoes. Ensure that still water is changed regularly and use effective mosquito repellents if necessary.

Winter sports are well loved by many, but be sure to be warmly dressed to prevent hypothermia.

and short-lasting—such as soreness at the site of injection, occasional fever and fatigue.

The above information is meant as a general guideline. You should consult your doctor as to whether you are a candidate for viral hepatitis vaccinations.

THIRD TRAVEL STORY

Tom was an expatriate Canadian engineer who was working in Singapore on the construction of a new mass rapid transit system. During his off days, he made it a point to visit as many Asian destinations as possible. After all, he thought, when would he get a chance to pass through this region again. In addition to exploring places of interest in Asia, he was adventurous in sampling the local exotic dishes. On a trip to Hong Kong, he indulged on a variety of local delicacies including century eggs, fish head curry, turtle soup and ducks feet. He was, however, meticulous in practising safe eating habits. He ate only food that was cooked or boiled. He did not drink the local water, but consumed only bottled beverages or freshly brewed tea. He tried many of the local fruit such as durian, mangoesteen, rambutan and lychee, all of which could be peeled.

Yes, Tom was exceptionally cautious, or at least he thought so. However, he was unaware that one of the local dishes, the barbecued clams had not been adequately cooked. Clams, as most of the mollusc family, thrive in water contaminated with organic pollutants such as sewage. Throughout the world, they are a common source of bacterial and viral disease.

Unknown to Tom was that clams and mussels are usually not completely cooked in Asia. The reason being that cooking makes them chewy and not delectable for local taste. As it turned out, the clams he ate were contaminated with the hepatitis A virus. The virus is endemic throughout most parts of Asia and the majority of Asians have developed immunity since early childhood. Hepatitis A infections during childhood are usually mild and most of the time undetected. However, contracting this virus during adulthood, as in Tom's case, can be associated with a more virulent infection.

Unfortunately, Tom became very sick six weeks after leaving Hong Kong. He initially developed fever, muscle aches, nausea and generalised weakness. Then, his urine turned a dark tea colour and his skin (and eyes) became yellow. His appetite was poor and he began to vomit. There was no choice but to admit him to a hospital and rehydrate him with intravenous fluids. Since hepatitis A is caused by a virus, antibiotics are useless. Therefore, only supportive medical care could be given to Tom. Gradually, his own immune defences were able to eradicate the virus from his liver. He was discharged after spending a week in the hospital. However, it was another two weeks before he could return to work and another six weeks before his stamina returned to normal.

The only positive aspect of Tom's illness was that he developed life-long immunity to the hepatitis A virus. However, this had occurred at a substantial cost of his time and money.

The lesson of this tragedy is clear. Tourists beware!

MALARIA

CHAPTER 7

'That is your trick, your bit of filthy magic:
invisibility, and the anaesthetic power to
deaden my attention in your direction.'
—D.H. Lawrence, *The Mosquito*

Suffering from Side Effects

Jim was not himself. He was dizzy and lethargic. His sense of balance was impaired and he had difficulty walking a straight line. He had trouble coordinating his fingers and was unable to button his shirt or even tie his shoe laces. Then, a few days later, he developed vertigo, vomiting and was too weak to get out of bed.

—A backpacker suffering from the neurological side effects of an antimalarial medication

SYMPTOMS, TREATMENT AND PREVENTION

Malaria is a tropical disease of humans caused by four species of the Plasmodium parasite. Other names for malaria, particularly used in European countries, are 'Paludism' or 'Paludeen fever'. All four types of the malaria parasite are transmitted by mosquitoes of the genus Anopheles. Most fatal infections are caused by the falciparum species and are more likely to occur when diagnosis and treatment are delayed or inappropriate.

Malaria is a worldwide problem because two-thirds of the world's population lives in malaria endemic regions. A conservative estimate is that there are 220 million new infections a year. In Africa alone, malaria causes over a million deaths each year. The problem has become worse in recent times because of mosquitoes becoming increasingly resistance to pesticides, and because of increasing drug resistance of the malaria parasites.

How Can One Avoid Malaria Infections?

If you are planning a trip to an endemic area, you should be made aware of the following:

- Most tourists confine their activities to major cities and towns where the risk of contracting malaria is low. Therefore, in these circumstances, antimalarial drug prophylaxis is usually not necessary.
- Malaria is spread by mosquitoes which bite mainly at dusk and throughout the night. Therefore, avoid going out during these times.
- Any measures that reduce mosquito bites reduce the risk of contracting malaria, dengue fever, filariasis and other mosquito-transmitted diseases. Do not apply perfume or cologne and avoid wearing dark coloured clothing since they may attract mosquitoes. Use sprays, nets, screens and wear clothing with long sleeves and long pants. Use insect repellents containing at least 30 per

cent diethyltoluamide (DEET), especially during evening and night hours (please note that DEET can cause severe reactions particularly with prolonged or excessive use in children or in higher concentrations). Spraying clothing and shoes with permethrin (Permanone), and using permethrin-impregnated mosquito nets will also help keep mosquitoes away. Clothing that has been pre-treated with premethrin are commercially available. Please see the section on prevention against mosquito-borne disease for further advice.

- For prophylactic drugs to be effective, they must be taken regularly. However, prophylactic medication does not offer absolute protection against malaria. Furthermore, exceeding the recommended dosage of prophylactic medicine does not increase its effectiveness and may actually increase the risk of side effects. Therefore, all measures to prevent mosquitoe bites remain paramount.

What Type of Anti-malarial Prophylactic Drugs are Recommended?

This is a difficult and controversial area, but all international experts agree that some form of prophylaxis in endemic regions is necessary. The following general recommendations can be made, but are not intended to replace consultation with a doctor or public health department:

- In areas where there is no resistance to anti-malarial medication, chloroquine alone is sufficient. However, chloroquine resistance (primarily of the falciparum species) occurs in most endemic regions, especially Southeast Asia.
- Atovaquine/proguanil (Malarone) is a combination of two medications to prevent malaria. The tablet should be taken once daily starting one to two days before entering an endemic region, and to continue until seven days after leaving the endemic regions. The medication is well tolerated, and side effects are minimal (primarily nausea). This medication can also be used for self-treatment if

access to medical care is not available. The treatment dose is four tablets as a single dose for three consecutive days. Self-treatment is only a temporary measure. Urgent professional medical ad is recommended during or immediately after treatment

- Mefloquine is an alternative prophylactic medication for travelling within endemic falciparum regions. However, the medication should not be used for those whose occupation requires finger dexterity, fine coordination or spatial judgement. The medication is also contraindicated for those with a history of epilepsy, heart arrhythmias or psychiatric disorders. . Mefloquine is not recommended for children weighing less than 15 kg.

- Doxycycline is a long-acting antibiotic of the tetracycline group. It is recommended for those who will be at immediate risk for malaria and therefore unable to start anti-malarial prophylaxis a week prior to exposure (e.g. oil field engineers travelling at short notice into the jungles). Doxycycline is also recommended where Mefloquine resistance has been reported (e.g. the Thai-Cambodian border region). Tetracycline should not be taken by pregnant women or children younger than eight years of age because of adverse effects on developing teeth and bones.

Pregnant women should avoid travelling in malaria endemic regions. If this is not possible, then the following medications to prevent malaria may be taken after consultation with your doctor:

- Chloroquine phosphate may be taken if entering a region where malaria is sensitive to chloroquine phosphate. This medication is reported to be safe to the fetus if taken in the recommended prophylactic dosage for an adult.

- Mefloquine may be taken during the second and third trimester if entering a region where malaria is resistant to chloroquine. According to the CDC, 'more limited data suggest it is also safe during the first trimester'.

Please note that taking medication regularly and appropriately will not completely prevent getting a malaria infection. Therefore, it is imperative to consult your doctor if fever or flu-like symptoms develop during or after travelling in an endemic region.

A list of anti-malarial prophylactic drugs and their dosage is provided below. However, before leaving one's country to visit a malaria endemic area, it is best to consult with your doctor or government health department for specific recommendations.

DRUGS USED IN THE PROPHYLAXIS OF MALARIA
(reprinted from the U. S. Centers for Disease Control and Prevention)

Drug	Usage	Adult dose	Pediatric dose	Comments
Atovaquone/ proguanil (Malarone™)	Prophylaxis in all areas	Adult tablets contain 250 mg atovaquone and 100 mg proguanil hydrochloride 1 adult tablet orally, daily	Pediatric tablets contain 62.5 mg atovaquone and 25 mg proguanil hydrochloride 5-8 kg: $^1/_2$ pediatric tablet daily ≥8-10 kg: $^3/_4$ pediatric tablet daily ≥10-20 kg: 1 pediatric tablet daily ≥20-30 kg: 2 pediatric tablets daily ≥30-40 kg: 3 pediatric tablets daily ≥40 kg: 1 adult tablet daily (Updated 22 December 2006)	Begin 1–2 days before travel to malarious areas. Take daily at the same time each day while in the malarious area, and for 7 days after leaving such areas. Contraindicated in persons with severe renal impairment (creatinine clearance < 30mL/min). Atovaquone/ proguanil should be taken with food or a milky drink. Not recommended for children < 5 kg, pregnant women, and women breastfeeding infants weighing < 5 kg. (Updated 22 December 2006)

Chloroquine phosphate (Aralen™ and generic)	Prophylaxis only in areas with chloroquine-sensitive malaria	300 mg base (500 mg salt) orally, once/week	5 mg/kg base (8.3 mg/kg salt) orally, once/week, up to maximum adult dose of 300mg base	Begin 1–2 weeks before travel to malarious areas. Take weekly on the same day of the week while in the malarious areas and for 4 weeks after leaving such areas. May exacerbate psoriasis.
Doxycycline (Many brand names and generic)	Prophylaxis in all areas	100 mg orally, daily	8 years of age or more: 2 mg/kg up to adult dose of 100mg/day	Begin 1–2 days before travel to malarious areas. Take daily at the same time each day while in the malarious area and for 4 weeks after leaving such areas. Contraindicated in children < 8 years of age and pregnant women.
Hydro-xychloroquine sulfate (Plaquenil™)	An alternative to chloroquine for primary prophylaxis* only in areas with chloroquine-sensitive malaria	310 mg base (400 mg salt) orally, once/week	5 mg/kg base (6.5 mg/kg salt) orally, once/week, up to maximum adult dose of 310 mg base	Begin 1–2 weeks before travel to malarious areas. Take weekly on the same day of the week while in the malarious areas and for 4 weeks after leaving such areas. May exacerbate psoriasis.
Mefloquine (Lariam™ and generic)	Prophylaxis in areas with mefloquine-sensitive malaria	228 mg base (250 mg salt) orally, once/week	≤9 kg: 4.6 mg/kg base (5 mg/kg salt) orally, once/week

10-19 kg: ¼ tablet once/week

20-30 kg: ½ tablet, once/week

31-45 kg: ¾ tablet once/week

≥46 kg: 1 tablet, once/week | Begin 1–2 weeks before travel to malarious areas. Take weekly on the same day of the week while in the malarious areas and for 4 weeks after leaving such areas. Contraindicated in persons allergic to mefloquine or related compounds (e.g. quinine and quinidine) and in persons with active depression, a recent history of depression, |

				generalised anxiety disorder, psychosis, schizophrenia, other major psychiatric disorders, or seizures. Use with caution in persons with psychiatric disturbances or a previous history of depression. Not recommended for persons with cardiac conduction abnormalities.
Primaquine	An option for prophylaxis in special circumstances. Call Malaria Hotline (770-488-7788) for additional information	30 mg base (52.6 mg salt) orally, daily	0.5 mg/kg base (0.8 mg/kg salt) up to adult dose, orally, daily	Begin 1–2 days before travel to malarious areas. Take daily at the same time each day while in the malarious area and for 7 days after leaving such areas. Contraindicated in persons with G6PD1 deficiency. Also contraindicated during pregnancy and lactation unless the infant being breast-fed has a documented normal G6PD level. Use in consultation with malaria experts.
Primaquine	Used for presumptive anti-relapse therapy (terminal prophylaxis) to decrease the risk of relapses of P. vivax and P. ovale	30 mg base (52.6 mg salt) orally, once/day for 14 days after departure from the malarious area	0.5 mg/kg base (0.8) mg/kg salt) up to adult dose orally, once/day for 14 days after departure from the malarious area	Indicated for persons who have had prolonged exposure to P. vivax and P. ovale or both. Contraindicated in persons with G6PD(1) deficiency. Also contraindicated during pregnancy and lactation unless the infant being breast-fed has a documented normal G6PD level.

(1) Glucose-6-phosphate dehydrogenase. All persons who take primaquine should have a documented normal G6PD level prior to starting the medication.

FOURTH TRAVEL STORY

When travelling in tropical countries, check with your doctor whether antimalarial drug prophylactics are necessary.

Forgetting to take proper antimalarial prophylactic medication is a frequent cause of illness among tourists, and occasionally death. One case that I recall vividly involved a young man named Bob. He was an American college student who went trekking in Bali, Indonesia, during his summer vacation. While there, he also visited some of the other nearby islands and by all accounts was having a marvellous time. Then, about six weeks after his arrival, he suddenly began having fever, muscle aches, headaches and profound lethargy. He initially started taking analgesic pills to reduce his fever and muscle aches. However, after his symptoms persisted for several days, he consulted a local Balinese doctor After a brief examination, he was given reassurance that his symptoms were most likely the result of a flu-like illness and that he should rest and drink plenty of fluids during the next couple of days.

Bob took the doctor's advice, but after a couple of days, his symptoms had become worse. He was too weak to walk, his appetite was poor and his fever was now unrelenting. Not only that, his urine had become a dark tea colour and his skin and eyes were turning yellow (jaundice).

His friends had to help carry him back to reconsult with the doctor. In view of his weakened state, poor appetite, dark tea colour urine and progressive jaundice, a preliminary diagnosis of hepatitis was made, and he was admitted to a local Balinese hospital.

While in the hospital, he was treated for presumed hepatitis. Although he was dehydrated from fever, nausea and vomiting, no intravenous fluids were given and meals had to be brought to him by his friends. Laboratory tests were done but medical facilities were limited.

Bob's condition deteriorated to the point that he became comatose and his kidneys ceased to function. His situation was now critical, and his friends contacted the regional American Consulate for assistance. Unfortunately, not being an employee of the State Department, there was not much they could do for him. However, the consulate was able to contact his family and provided them with the telephone number of a medical assistance company operating within the area.

After consulting with the medical assistance company, the family agreed that Bob should immediately be evacuated by plane to the nearest centre of medical excellence, which was Singapore.

After arriving in Singapore, he was admitted to an intensive care unit at a private hospital. Blood tests were taken which revealed that he was actually suffering from a deadly malaria strain!

The reason Bob was jaundice was because of an extensive destruction of his red blood cells by the malaria parasite, and not the result of liver impairment such as hepatitis.

He was immediately treated with appropriate intravenous antimalarial medication, and started on hemodialysis because of his kidney failure.

I am only too happy to say that Bob, after three weeks in the hospital and at a great medical expense, has recovered and has since returned to the United States. During his hospital stay, Bob disclosed that he had not been taking any antimalarial prophylactics while visiting some of the nearby islands where malaria was endemic.

Clearly, this near fatal tragedy illustrates several points. First, always take antimalarial medication when travelling in endemic regions. Secondly, it is a good idea to check with your health insurance company as to whether your policy also provides medical assistance when travelling. Medical assistance coverage will help you find competent doctors and can provide you with invaluable medical advice. While medical insurance by itself will only help pay for your medical costs after you return home. That is, if you return! A medical assistance company can help you get started on the right course of treatment, and therefore may circumvent more heroic measures such as air-lifts and evacuations. When travelling in underdeveloped regions with inadequate diagnostic facilities, symptoms of disease can be misleading. In this particular case, Bob's symptoms of jaundice, fever, loss of appetite, and fatigue were misinterpreted as the result of hepatitis. Therefore, a word for the wise is to include international medical assistance coverage as part of your overseas travel plans.

OTHER MOSQUITO AND INSECT-BORNE DISEASES
Dengue

For some mosquito transmitted diseases, there are no known drug treatments or vaccines, so prevention becomes extremely important. This is certainly true for dengue fever, which occurs widely in the tropical regions.

Dengue (also called breakbone fever) occurs about five to eight days after being bitten by an aedes mosquito infected with the virus. Classic symptoms include severe splitting headaches, high fever, backache, muscle and joint pains and skin rashes. The symptoms last from five to seven days.

Occasionally, the illness is complicated by a bleeding tendency and is then called dengue haemorrhagic fever, which sometimes can be fatal. In addition to the symptoms mentioned above, patients may also develop bruises and bleeding of the skin, nose and gums. Intestinal as well as other types of internal bleeding can occur.

Although treatment is entirely symptomatic, it is important to consult your doctor early to prevent complications. For those most symptomatic, hospital care may be needed. Treatment includes oral or intravenous fluid replacement, analgesics, fever medicine and close observation of vital parameters. Salicylates such as aspirin should not be given since they may aggravate bleeding tendencies. In cases complicated by dengue haemorrhagic fever (or shock), transfusion of blood and other blood products (such as platelets) may be necessary.

Since there are at least four different strains of dengue virus, recovering from one type of dengue infection does not provide immunity against the others. Furthermore, secondary dengue infections can increase the risk of haemorrhagic complications. Trials for a vaccine against dengue fever are being carried out in Southeast Asia under the direction of the World Health Organisation. At present, preliminary trials have shown the vaccine to be safe and effective in developing immunity against all four strains of the dengue virus. The vaccine may be commercially available for worldwide use in five years.

Chikungunya Fever

Our world is getting smaller, but for transmitted diseases it is getting bigger. We live in an age of incessant travel. Travel to remote parts of the world and contact with diverse people groups is expanding exponentially. Unfortunately, this has brought about the dissemination of communicable diseases to areas outside of their historical endemic regions. Among these diseases is chikungunya fever. In years past, chikungunya fever was a disease primarily of the African continent. But gradually, this disease has been introduced into Asia and now poses a substantial health issue.

Symptoms

Chikungunya fever is caused by the chikungunya virus, which is spread by the bite of the Aedes mosquito. This type of mosquito is prevalent throughout Southeast Asia including Singapore. After an infected mosquito bites, the incubation period varies from one to twelve days (typically three to seven). The symptoms of Chikungunaya fever are very similar to dengue, consisting of fever, chills, headache, low back pain, nausea, vomiting and rash. In addition, pain and inflammation of the joints may occur. The symptoms can last from three to ten days, although the join pains may last several weeks. In most cases the illness is self-limiting, and rarely fatal. Clinical diagnosis can be confirmed by blood test.

Treatment

Similar to dengue, there is no vaccine or drug to treat chikungunya fever. Treatment is primarily symptomatic consisting of bed rest, drinking fluids, and taking either paracetamol or acetaminophen to reduce fever, headache or joint aches. Medication to relieve nausea or vomiting may also be needed. Aspirin and non-steroidal anti-inflammatory medication (such as ibuprofen and naproxen) should be avoided, since they may cause stomach discomfort (gastritis) and internal bleeding in those who may also have dengue fever. Some patients may need to be hospitalised for intravenous fluids if oral hydration is not adequate.

Any measures that reduce mosquito breeding and mosquito bites are paramount. Symptomatic persons should be kept at home until the fever has resolved. They also should be isolated from mosquitoes to reduce transmission to household members. This may be accomplished by the use of mosquito sprays, nets and coils, or staying in a closed air-conditioned environment.

Prevention of Mosquito-borne Disease

If you plan to travel or reside in mosquito-infested regions, the following measures are recommended to reduce the chances of getting mosquito-borne diseases (including malaria, filariasis, Japanese encephalitis, Ross River fever, Chikunganya, Rift Valley fever, dengue, yellow fever and many others).

- If you are not staying in a closed, air-conditioned facility, then correct use of mosquito nets is important. For added protection (up to three months or longer), mosquito nets can be soaked in a one per cent solution of permethrin or other insect repellent. If you plan to reside in a malaria endemic area, the curtains can be treated in a similar manner. All windows and doors should be screened and all cracks in the building sealed.

- Pyrethroid mosquito coils can be used if mosquito nets are not available. These coils are impregnated with pyrethrum. The effectiveness of mosquito coils not containing pyrethrum is questionable. Electronic (cigarette-lighter type) repellents, which are supposed to work by emitting a high-frequency whine, do not discourage mosquitoes from biting.

- 'Knockdown' insecticide sprays (not insect repellents) can be used to spray the sleeping areas every night.

- Wear clothing with long sleeves and long pants during the evening and at night. Avoid wearing dark-coloured clothing and using perfume or cologne, since all of these attract mosquitoes.

- Use effective mosquito repellents that contain at least 30 per cent diethyltoluamide (DEET) on exposed skin and clothing especially during evening and night hours. However, concentrations of DEET above 50 per cent are not more effective, and sometimes can cause reactions. Apply DEET repellents sparingly and only to exposed skin. Prolong and excessive use, especially in children, should be avoided. Avoid inhaling or swallowing DEET. Also, avoid getting it on eyes, sores or rashes. These repellents must be reapplied regularly to maintain their effectiveness. However, wash them off when coming indoors when their protection is no longer needed. Rolled-on (deodorant-type) repellents work well on exposed parts of the body but cannot be applied to clothing. Since mosquitoes can bite through clothing, roll-ons are not recommended. Other effective repellents include: a) Picaridin (KBR 3023, aka Bayrepel, and icaridin outside the US, Chemical Name: 2-(2-hydroxyethyl)-1-piperidinecarboxylic acid 1-methylpropyl ester) Products containing picaridin include but are not limited to: Cutter Advanced, Skin so

THAT'S YOUR MOTHER'S NEW MOSQUITO KILLER

Soft Bug Guard Plus and Autan (outside the US) b) Oil of lemon Eucalyptus or PMD c) IR3535 Chemical Name: 3-[N-Butyl-N-acetyl]-aminopropionic acid, ethyl ester) Products containing IR3535 include but are not limited to: Skin so Soft Bug Guard Plus Expedition.

- Use an electric fan at night to discourage mosquitoes from settling.
- Remove standing water of all forms around the area to eliminate potential breeding habitats of mosquitoes.
- Regular fogging is recommended in order to kill resting mosquitoes in dwellings and the surrounding environment.

These measures will substantially reduce but not eliminate the risk of mosquito-borne diseases. These measures should be combined with the use of appropriate medication to prevent malaria when travelling in endemic areas.

Yellow Fever

Yellow fever is a viral infection transmitted by mosquitoes (primarily the Aedes type). It is endemic in the regions of tropical South America and most of Africa between 15°North and 15°South. The disease is transmitted by mosquitoes in two basically different cycles, urban (human-mosquito-human) and jungle (primate-mosquito-human).

The incubation period for yellow fever is usually three to six days. Initial symptoms include intense headache, fever, nausea, vomiting, muscle aches and generalised weakness. However, some cases progressed to more serious complications including bleeding disorders, liver and kidney impairment, delirium and death. Only symptomatic and supportive treatment is available. Therefore, vaccination and preventative measures are essential. The vaccination is given as a single dose of live virus vaccine at registered vaccination centres which will issue a certificate of vaccination. The vaccination and certificate are good for ten years. Side effects of the vaccine are usually mild and short-lasting and consist of muscle aches, mild fever and headache. Since yellow fever vaccine is produced using chick embryos, it should be given cautiously to individuals allergic to eggs.

Since it is a 'live virus vaccine', the vaccine is not recommended for children below nine months or immunosuppressed patients (those with leukaemia, cancer, taking steroids, receiving chemotherapy or who have AIDS) unless approved by a doctor.

Typhus Fever

Typhus fever is a general term comprising a group of rickettsial diseases that are transmitted by fleas, mites and body louse. These diseases occur wherever an infected rodent population (rats, mice, squirrels) live in close proximity to humans.

Scrub typhus is limited to Eastern and South-eastern Asia, India, Australia and adjacent islands. Endemic typhus fever is found throughout the world wherever fleas and rats abound. Epidemic typhus is rare except when municipal services are disrupted such as during war and disasters.

Symptoms of the different types of typhus are similar and consist of fever, headache and rashes.

Antibiotic treatment (either tetracycline or chloramphenicol) is effective in eradicating the infection. There are no satisfactory vaccines. However, prevention in highly infested areas can be achieved by the application of insect repellents to clothing and skin.

Leishmaniasis

Leishmaniasis is caused by the protozoan parasite Leishmania. It is transmitted to humans by sandfly bites. Transmission can also occur by transfusion from infected blood donors. There are two major manifestations of the disease, internal organ injury (also called visceral or Kala azar) and cutaneous (skin infection).

The visceral form is characterised by recurrent fevers, weight loss, low blood counts, liver and spleen enlargement, generalised weakness and ultimately death. It is endemic in China, Russia, India, the Middle East, Egypt, eastern half of Africa (from the Sahara in the north to the equator in the south) and Latin America. The incubation period is generally about three months (but may vary from three weeks to 18 months).

Cutaneous Leishmaniasis is characterised by lesions (single or multiple) on exposed areas of the skin that usually ulcerate. This type of leishmaniasis is found in areas bordering the Mediterranean, the Middle East, India, South and Central America. The incubation period varies from two to 24 months.

Treatment of all forms of Leishmaniasis is with antimonial medications. There is no effective vaccine or prophylatic drugs. Prevention is by applying insect repellents, preferably containing DEET, to expose areas of the body especially during evening and night hours (the feeding time of the sandfly). The repellent must be applied regularly to maintain its effectiveness. Spraying clothing with permethrin (permanone) and using permethrin-impregnated mosquito nets may also help. Very fine mosquito bed netting and window screens are necessary since the sandfly is very small (only one-third the size of a mosquito).

Trypanosomiasis

There are two different types of trypanosomiasis, Chaga's disease (also called American trypanosomiasis) and sleeping sickness (also called African trypanosomiasis).

Chaga's Disease

Chaga's disease is caused by the protozoan parasite Trypanosoma cruzi. The disease is found only in the Americas, ranging from the southern United States to Southern Argentina. It is transmitted to humans by the bite of the reduviid bugs. As in Leishmaniasis, the disease can sometimes be transmitted by blood transfusion from infected donors.

The incubation period is about one week. At the site of the insect bite, skin swelling and redness occurs (often referred to as a chagoma) associated with enlargement of the regional lymph glands. This skin lesion is sometimes followed by systemic symptoms such as fever, lethargy, generalised lymph gland swelling and liver and spleen enlargement. Serious complications include infection of the heart muscles which can lead to heart failure.

Following resolution of the initial symptoms, the organism often persists in a dormant phase. During this chronic, dormant infestation, a minority of individuals will develop chronic heart and intestinal disorders that sometimes lead to death.

Treatment for Chaga's disease is not satisfactory. Medications such as nifurtimox and benznidazole help minimise the complications of the disease but do not eradicate it. Since there are no effective drugs nor vaccines, preventative measures are even more important. When travelling in endemic regions, travellers should avoid sleeping in dilapidated dwellings, especially those with thatched roofs. Insect repellents and fine netting provide additional protection.

Sleeping Sickness

This form of trypanosomiasis is caused by the protozoan Trypanosoma brucei and is transmitted by the African tsetse fly. The disease is endemic in tropical Africa between 15°North and 20°South latitude. A painful chancre occurs at the site of entry, later followed by fever, lethargy and headache.

If the infection is left untreated, neurologic symptoms may begin months or years later (including balance impairment, tremors, sleepiness, coma and death). Drugs such as suramin and pentamidine are effective if treatment is started early. However, they can be associated with serious side effects and must be administered under the direction of a physician.

There is no vaccine against sleeping sickness.

Travellers to rural areas or national game reserves should avoid areas known by the local inhabitants to be of risk.

The tsete fly bites during the day. It is the size of a honey bee and is capable of biting through light-weight clothing. Applying insect repellent, preferably containing DEET, to skin and clothing is advisable.

Onchocerciasis (River Blindness)

Onchocerciasis is caused by a filarial worm parasite which is transmitted by the bite of the female blackfly (Simulium species). There are an estimated 20 million people infected with onchocerciasis, the vast majority of whom live within equatorial Africa in a belt that stretches from the Atlantic to the Red Sea.

Other smaller endemic areas include Guatemala, Mexico, Venezuela, Columbia, Brazil, Ecuador, Yemen and Saudi Arabia.

The major complications of this disease are blindness and skin damage (loss of elasticity, pigmentation changes and wrinkling).

Ivermectin is now considered the drug of choice for treating onchocerciasis. However, it cannot be given to pregnant women, women who are breastfeeding or children under the age of five.

There are no vaccine or prophylactic medication to protect against infection.

Prevention is best achieved by avoiding areas known to be infested such as along free-flowing rivers and streams during the morning and evening hours.

Protective clothing and the use of insect repellents containing DEET is also advisable.

Plague

Plague is a disease caused by the bacterium Yersinia pestis which is transmitted by rodent fleas. Plague is described

Urban epidemics of plague are uncommon. However, recently there was an outbreak in the Maharashtra and Gujarat states in the Western part of India.. However, rural cases of plague still occur in south-western United States, widely scattered areas of South America, in north-central, eastern and southern Africa, Iranian Kardistan, Yemen, Saudi Arabia, Central and Southeast Asia (Myanmar, China, Indonesia, Mongolia, Vietnam and the eastern part of Russia).

as being bubonic (lymph glands), pneumonic (lungs) and septicaemica (blood) depending on its mode of entry into the body. The bubonic form typically occurs when rat fleas first bite an infected rat, and then later transmit the disease by biting humans. The plague can also infect hunters who skin infected rodents and cut the meat into pieces. Transmission apparently occurs by the bacterium directly penetrating the skin through visible (or invisible) sores or cuts. Symptoms of the bubonic plague include headache, generalise weakness, fever, shaking chills, pain and swollen glands at the site of infection. The pneumonic plague is much more virulent and may be fatal unless treated with antibiotics. It is transmitted to others by the cough of a person who has infection involving the lung.

The risk of infection to travellers in these areas is extremely low. This is especially true if someone is visiting only urban areas and staying in modern hotels.

There is a vaccine against plague, but it only provides limited, short-term immunity (up to six months). Since revaccination is associated with adverse side effects, it is recommended only for high-risk groups such as laboratory personal doing research on the plague or field workers in endemic regions. However, travellers briefly visiting a plague endemic area may protect themselves by taking either tetracycline or co-trimoxazole.

Hikers and outdoor-bound people in endemic areas should be warned of the dangers of plague. They should not touch or caress sick rodents. Also, their pets should be restrained and powdered with flea repellents.

Diseases Caused by Ticks

Ticks are blood-sucking insects that are responsible for many infectious diseases throughout the world.

The diseases inflicted by ticks include Rocky Mountain spotted fever, Q fever, tularemia, borreliosis, human babesiosis and Lyme disease.

In addition to the disease they carry, tick bites can result in localised skin reactions and itching, and secondary bacterial infections. If the head and mouth parts are not completely removed, persistent inflammation of the surrounding skin can result in a painful, itching nodule that may need surgical excision. Some ticks also inject a potent neurotoxin while feeding which can result in paralysis. Removal of the tick will prevent as well as reverse the paralysis.

Ticks can live in diverse habitats but are most commonly found in woody and grassland environments. They climb bushes and jump unto warm-blooded animals straying their way. They then penetrate the skin with a long syringe-like proboscis and feed on blood.

Two diseases worth special mention are Lyme disease and Rocky Mountain spotted fever.

Lyme disease was discovered only recently (1975) in the north-eastern part of the United States. However, it is now recognised as a worldwide infection (wherever the Ixodid ticks inhabit). Many cases have been reported in the United States, throughout Europe (from Great Britain to Russia), Asia and Australia. Most of these cases occur during the summer months. Hikers, campers and outdoor people are particularly prone because of their activities in rural and wooded areas. Lyme disease is caused by a spirochete organism (Borrelia burdorferi). It is a member of the same family of diseases that causes syphilis. A few days after a tick bite, the organisms expand centrifugally, often producing an expanding, red ring-like skin reaction. Subsequently, the victim may develop fever, severe headaches, neck stiffness and even meningitis. If the disease is not promptly treated with antibiotics, long-term complications such as arthritis (and less commonly encephalitis) can occur.

Rocky Mountain spotted fever occurs primarily in the western hemisphere (the United States, Canada, Mexico, Brazil and Colombia). It is caused by the rickettsia organism

Rickettsia rickettsii. The incubation period following a tick bite is three to 12 days.

Symptoms consist of severe headache, fever, chills and muscle aches. A characteristic spotted rash appears on the extremities and body. Severe infections can result in confusion, delirium, shock, kidney failure and even death. The disease often responds to early treatment with a broad spectrum of antibiotics.

The best prevention against tick bites is to avoid entering tick-infested areas. However, this may not be a suitable solution to many people. Other measures include wearing long sleeve shirts and long pants. Shirts should also be tucked in, and similarly pants tucked inside the boots. Insect repellents containing DEET should be applied to exposed skin. Clothing can also be impregnated with insect repellents containing either DEET or permethrin. After each day outdoors, it is a good idea to inspect the body for ticks (including the head and hairy regions). If a tick is found, it is important to remove the tick entirely and not to leave the mouth parts of the head behind. This is best accomplished by using a pair of fine tweezers and applying gentle but persistent pressure to the tick's head until it lets go. Other measures include applying a drop of oil, petroleum, nail polish or organic solvent onto the tick. Do not apply heat or a burning cigarette since it will more likely harm the victim.

Finally, any person bitten by a tick should see a doctor if they become symptomatic (e.g. fever, chills, headache or malaise). Early treatment may prevent subsequent complications.

FIFTH TRAVEL STORY

Beware of mosquitoes! In the tropics, these blood-sucking parasites not only cause malaria but a whole host of viral diseases such as dengue fever, Japanese encephalitis and filariosis to name a few.

I am only too cognisant of the dangers mosquitoes can bring, ever since I myself was bitten by a mosquito which carried the dreaded dengue fever virus while vacationing in the Philippines. Dengue fever is also known as 'break bone fever' reflecting the intense suffering that occurs. Although it has been almost 13 years since my near tragic illness, I still can remember vividly the details of my ill-fated trip.

I took a four-week self-arranged vacation to the Philippines in July 1982. During the first week, I explored Manila, the capital of the Philippines, and its surrounding environs. The sprawling city was noisy, congested, polluted and teeming with humanity. After visiting most of the major attractions, riding the crowded 'jeepneys' and revelling in the vibrant night life until the wee morning hours, I decided it was time to get away from the frenzied pace of Manila and explore some of the serene tropical islands. After all, the Philippines has over 7,000 of them!. I took a ferry to the village of Panay where I stayed overnight. I then took a large outrigger boat to the idyllic island of Boracay, renowned for its pristine white sandy beaches and clear water. Boracay, however, was not for the pampered, mass-market tourists since at that time there was no indoor plumbing, electricity or any other modern day creature comfort. Time, and diversions of 'civilisation' were not important on Boracay. I simply enjoyed the serenity, the sunsets, the beach strolls and most of all, the genuine, earthly hospitality of its people.

However, my week of sun, fun and solitude came to an abrupt halt four days after arrival. During an evening walk on the beach, I suddenly developed dizziness and had difficulty concentrating. I knew something was seriously wrong, but what? I hurried back to my nipa hut to rest. Then, on the following morning, my illness had taken a turn for the worse. I had a high grade fever, my body was drenched from sweat and my head felt as if someone had struck it with a hammer. To make matters worse, I had intense pain in the bones of my back, legs and arms as if they were 'being broken'.

Being a doctor, I suspected that I was suffering from a viral illness, perhaps hepatitis. However, here I was on an isolated island with absolutely no medical facilities, let alone electricity or telephones. I asked several local inhabitants for a doctor, but was shocked when they brought to my hut the village medicine man known locally as a *bomo*. However, I somehow managed to keep my wits. I knew that above all else, I had to keep myself hydrated. I therefore drank almost industrial quantities of coconut juice (which is an excellent isotonic solution rich in glucose and electrolytes). I took paracetamol tablets to reduce my fever and relieve my body aches and splitting headache. I avoided the hot sun and kept all necessary activities to the evening and morning hours. Furthermore, I made sure I had plenty of rest and sleep. Gradually my condition improved and after one week, I had regained enough stamina to leave the island by the same outrigger boat. One month later while recuperating, I visited the US Naval Hospital in Subic Bay. There blood tests were done which confirmed that my recent illness was the result of the dengue fever virus.

I completely recovered from my illness. Sometimes, however, dengue fever can be complicated by internal bleeding and even death. This sobering experience of being gravely ill on a remote and underdeveloped island had taught me a few hard-learned lessons. First, if you plan to travel to remote places, be prepared for medical emergencies and pack a well supplied medical kit. If you develop a febrile illness or diarrhoea, try to drink plenty of fluids to avoid dehydration. A good guide as to adequate hydration is to keep the colour of your urine closer to that of water, and not of dark yellow. Use mosquito sprays or ointment where skin is exposed. After dusk, wear long sleeves and pants to reduce the chances of getting mosquito-borne diseases. Finally, it is best to travel with a friend when visiting remote areas. You never know when a sudden illness or accident may strike!

SIXTH TRAVEL STORY

Ralph, a 33-year-old surveyor from New Zealand, worked for a multinational lumber company in Kalimantan (formerly Borneo). Because of the nature of his work, he spent most of his time in Kalimantan, living in its rural areas and small villages. He was well aware of the risk of malaria, which was endemic within the region, and took his weekly antimalarial medications as directed. He felt reassured that the medications would protected him from malaria carrying mosquitoes that fly in swarms along the river banks. He heard of horror stories concerning others, less careful, who did not take antimalarial prophylactics.

Ralph remained relatively healthy and very busy supervising the logging operation. However, on a couple of occasions, he did feel feverish and had muscle aches But these discomforts were short lasting and never a concern to Ralph. Then, insidiously he noticed progressive swelling of both lower legs. He did not feel pain and he had no fever. Except for the swelling, he felt generally well and was able to continue with his work. However, there was no abatement of the swelling during the following week and he became very concerned. The swelling had now extended from both lower legs up to the groin and also involved his scrotum. His legs were heavy and walking cumbersome. Ralph's company's managing director made arrangements for him to fly to the nearest centre of medical expertise, which happened to be Singapore.

After arrival, he was seen by a physician experienced in tropical diseases. Being a young, active male with no history of prior medical problems, cardiac and renal disease were quickly ruled out as a cause of the swelling. A chest X-ray and abdominal scan were done but reported as normal. Laboratory tests were also essentially normal, except for a peculiar elevation of his eosinophil blood cell count. These types of cells become active and proliferate in response to parasitic infections. Special serology tests were therefore ordered which confirmed that Ralph was suffering from a microfilarial infection. Ralph was informed that this illness was transmitted by mosquitoes and that antimalarial prophylactics do not provide protection against this disease. The doctor explained that after the larvae stage of the parasite enters the blood stream, it migrates into the lymph gland drainage system. There, it matures into a slender worm-like organism that can grow up to 8–10 cm in length. The microfilarial worm inflames and obstructs normal lymphatic drainage, thereby causing massive swelling of the lower legs and/or scrotum. A common layman's term for the disease is 'elephantiasis', reflecting the massive enlargement of the extremities (or scrotum) that occurs. The disease is endemic throughout Southeast Asia, equatorial Africa, the Indian subcontinent, the Eastern Mediterranean region, the Western Pacific, South and Central America and the Caribbean.

Ralph was told that since there was no effective prophylactic medication or vaccine, preventative measures were paramount. These measures were explained to Ralph in detail since he planned to continue working within endemic areas.

Ralph was started on oral medications to be taken for at least three weeks. He was told that complete eradication of these worms was sometimes difficult and that repeated treatments may be necessary.

Fortunately for Ralph, his initial treatment was successful, and he has since returned to work in the tropics. However, Ralph has learned the limitations of medications and vaccinations in preventing tropical diseases. Since his illness, he has become more self-reliant and has taken it upon himself to practise measures that will reduce the chances of contracting insect-borne diseases. As he tells his colleagues, "bite prevention is more important than drugs".

SEXUALLY TRANSMITTED DISEASES

CHAPTER 8

'Physicians of the utmost fame were called at once. But
when they came, they answered as they took their fees,
"there is no cure for this disease".'
—Hilaire Belloc

A Personal Problem

He arrived at the doctor's office in a state of panic. In his haste, he had not scheduled an appointment. The receptionist asked in a pleasant voice, "Can I help you sir?" "Yes," he anxiously replied. "I need to see the doctor urgently, it's a personal problem".

—A middle-age businessman suffering the consequences of a close encounter of the worse kind

TRANSMISSION, TREATMENT AND PREVENTION

Unfortunately, the above scenario at the doctor's office is a common occurrence.

The World Health Organisation estimates that there are 365,000 new cases of sexually transmitted diseases everyday. Sexually transmitted diseases (STD) can be a major health hazard to the promiscuous traveller. The list of STD include not only the venerable venereal diseases like syphilis, viral hepatitis, gonorrhoea, chancoid and genital warts, but also a 'new generation' of disease such as non-specific urethritis and the AIDS virus (HIV).

STD are usually transmitted by sexual contact with an infected person. However, STD can also be transmitted by contact with open weepy sores, body fluids, discharge or mucous membranes. STD can sometimes be transmitted by blood transfusions, especially in developing countries where screening measures are inadequate. STD *are not* transmitted by toilet seats, hand towels, door handles or casual contact since these organism die quickly outside the body. Furthermore, STD, including the HIV virus, are not transmitted by mosquitoes or other insects.

COMMON TYPES OF STD
Gonorrhoea
The symptoms of gonorrhoea appear about three to five days after sexual intercourse with an infected person. The symptoms of men are either a thick (sometimes thin) discharge with pus, or a burning discomfort when urinating. However, up to 20 per cent of men may have no symptoms at all.

Women may have a vaginal discharge, burning urination or pelvic discomfort. Interestingly, up to 80 per cent of women may have no symptoms at all. Newborn babies, if delivered from an infected mother, will have a pus-like discharge from the eyes. If left untreated, the infection can lead to blindness.

Gonorrhoea can easily be diagnosed by microscopic examination of the discharge or by a laboratory culture. Traditionally, gonorrhoea was treated by penicillin, but the emergence of resistant strains has required more potent antibiotics.

Syphilis
This venereal infection is less common than gonorrhoea. The earliest symptoms may be a painless open sore on the male or female sex organ. Occasionally, a sore can be present on the lips, mouth, tongue or fingers. The secondary stage is manifested by rash or skin lesions (on parts or over the entire body), enlargement of the lymph glands or hair loss. If left untreated, syphilis can later lead to severe heart, brain and bone disease.

The initial stages of syphilis may be diagnosed by microscopic examination of tissue taken from a lesion. However, blood testing is usually required especially in diagnosing the secondary and late stages of syphilis where symptoms may be subtle. Treatment is by antibiotics.

Genital Herpes

This is a venereal virus infection. Initial infection is characterised by fever, headache, muscle pains, lymph gland enlargement in the groin and painful blisters on or near the sex organs. These symptoms will usually resolve within a couple of weeks. However, milder recurrent attacks can occur in up to 90 per cent of cases. Treatment is limited. Antiviral drugs such as acyclovir have been shown to speed the healing of lesions and resolution of symptoms, but are not curative. This medication, which is available in tablet form, is most effective for the initial (or primary) infection and less so for recurrent flare-ups.

Genital Warts

Genital warts (condylomata acuminata) are caused by the human papillomavirus and occur on the skin and mucosal surfaces of the external sex organs and anus. The incubation period is from one to six months after contact with an infected partner. Genital warts can be removed by applying caustic agents, interferon injections, surgery, freezing (cryosurgery) or ablation with laser. Frequently, the warts will recur regardless of the type of treatment.

Vaginitis

This is an infection of the vagina characterised by a foul smelling discharge, vaginal itching and sometimes painful urination. The most common organisms causing this condition are Trichomonas vaginalis, Candida albicans and Gardnerella vaginalis. Unlike the latter two organisms, Trichomonas is transmitted only by sexual contact.

Diagnosis is made by examination of vaginal secretions with a microscope. Treatment with metronidazole is usually effective against Trichomonas vaginalis and Gardnerella vaginalis. Sexual partners of those infected with Trochomonas vaginalis should also be treated concurrently, if recurrent infection is to be avoided. Candida infections can be treated with a single oral dose of fluconazole or with antifungal vaginal creams or pessaries.

Non-specific Urethritis

Non-specific urethritis (also called non-gonococcal urethritis) is caused by a diverse group of venereal pathogens. However, the majority are attributed to either the chlamydia or ureaplasma organisms. The symptoms of men include a thin, mucoid urethral discharge and burning urination. Infected women usually develop vaginal discharge, painful urination or pelvic pain. However as with other STD, many infected persons have no symptoms at all. Diagnosis can often be made by either culturing or detecting the antigen of the organism with a urethral or vaginal swab. Treatment is usually with antibiotics such as tetracycline, doxycycline or erythromycin for seven to ten days. A single dose of azithromycin (1 g orally) is an attractive albeit currently expensive alternative.

AIDS (Acquired Immunodeficiency Syndrome)

This emerging STD was first recognised 1981 after a group of gay men in the United States became ill with a rare type of cancer. Since then, AIDS has become a modern day plague, and an estimated 25 million deaths have occurred worldwide. According to the UNAIDS 2008 report, there were 2.7 million new HIV infections and two million HIV-related deaths in the year 2007. The CDC estimates that about one million people in the United States are living with HIV or AIDS. The good news is that in some countries in Asia, Latin American, and sub-Saharan Africa, the annual number of new HIV infections is falling. The number of AIDS cases in the United States began to fall dramatically in 1996.

The HIV virus slowly damages the immune system over years. In particular, the virus attacks and lowers the T cells or CD4 cells in the body, which are important to fight infection. Initially, people infected with the HIV virus feel and look good, and many continue to stay healthy for a number of years. With time, some develop AIDS-related conditions such as weight loss, recurrent diarrhoea, swollen glands, fever and lethargy. AIDS is the final stage of disease caused by the HIV virus. AIDS is diagnosed once someone has developed certain kinds of disease or certain types of cancer (such as Kaposi's sarcoma) associated with a very low T cell count.

The HIV virus is found in blood, semen and vaginal fluid of an infected person. Transmission occurs only by one of three ways: 1) having sex (anal, vaginal or oral) 2) sharing infected needles and syringes or 3) transmission of the virus to the fetus or infant during pregnancy, childbirth or by breast-feeding. Before the development of accurate testing, the HIV virus was transmitted through blood transfusion. Since the virus is fragile, it cannot live for long outside of its human host. Therefore, you cannot get AIDS from toilet seats, dishes and eating utensils, shaking hands, touching or a casual kiss. You also cannot get AIDS by mosquito or any other insect bite.

AIDS used to be a uniformably fatal disease. Fortunately, with the advent of antiretroviral drugs, lifespan with the disease has increased, and the death rate from HIV infection has fallen dramatically.

HOW TO PREVENT STD?

Abstinence, or having sex with only one sexual partner, and for both partners to remain mutually faithful to each other is the only foolproof method to prevent STD. If this is not possible, then limiting the number of sexual partners, using latex condoms with a lubricant, and periodic STD testing will reduce risk. Avoid getting high with drugs or alcohol, since this will lower your resolve to engage in risky sex. Do not have casual sex with strangers, or in exchange for money or drugs. Remember the acronym ABC: A = Abstinence, B = Be Faithful, C = Condoms.

If you think you have contracted a STD, then early consultation with a physician is important. Many STD can be treated and complications avoided. Whenever possible, treatment of the sexual partner(s) is advisable.

SEVENTH TRAVEL STORY

'Good old boy' Hank from Houston had been working for the past six years as an oil rigger in the South China Sea.

Platform drilling at sea was intense, stressful and dangerous work. Physical and burn injuries were always a concern. Therefore, maintaining strict safety standards was imperative. Hank and his fellow oil riggers certainly earned their pay. Hank worked on alternate months. During his off months, he would spend his time unwinding at Pattaya beach in Thailand. There he would be found with his boisterous buddies drinking beer, gambling and visiting the myriad girlie bars. Hank not only earned his pay, but also certainly spent it.

During his numerous 'close encounters of the lewd kind', he would try to practise safe sex. However, after several beers and mixed drinks, judgement would give way to more basic instincts. Good old boy Hank was just having a grand old time off from work, until one morning when he woke up with a problem. He initially felt a twinge, followed by a mild discomfort of his penis. He also noticed a slight mucoid discharge that stained his underwear. Hank paid little attention to this. But the following day, his penis started to throbbed with pain, and passing urine felt like fire. Hank quickly visited a nearby small medical clinic. The doctor told him not to worry and he was given a penicillin injection into the fleshy part of his buttocks as well as an assortment of medications. Hank waited a couple of days, but his symptoms only became worse. If his situation was not bad enough, he was devastated when his scrotum began to swell. Hank panicked. He took the next bus to Bangkok where he visited a specialist in venereal diseases. The specialist did blood tests and urethral discharge cultures. He was started on a tetracycline antibiotic and told to come back the following day. Hank had difficulty sleeping and developed an impending fear of doom. However, the following day, he was greatly relieved when the doctor told him that the test results demonstrated no evidence of AIDS or other life threatening disease. But the bad news was that he was suffering from Non-Specific Urethritis (NSU) caused by a highly virulent strain of chlamydia. These were alien terms to Hank. He just wanted to get rid of the damn bug!

The doctor explained to him that many of the chlamydia strains from the Pattaya and Bangkok regions were highly resistant to most antibiotics because of their liberal and widespread use. As a matter of fact, many of these antibiotics can be bought in Thailand without even a doctor's prescription! Hank was told that it would be necessary to treat him with two different types of antibiotics (erythromycin and a long-acting tetracycline). He would need to take these antibiotics for a long time (up to three or possibly four weeks) to ensure a complete cure. Hank was also told that sometimes untreated or repeated infections of this disease can result in long-term complications such as sterility and strictures of the penis. All this information was very disheartening to Hank. However, he thanked the doctor for being frank with him. He took both medications as prescribed and slowly his symptoms subsided. After three weeks, he was cured.

Hank had learned the hard way, the unforeseen horrors of casual and unsafe sex. He was no longer indiscriminate with his sexual encounters. He developed a steady relationship with only one woman. As a recent convert to practising safe sex, he fervently extols the lessons he learned: "If you cannot resist, at least use a condom. Otherwise, you may contract a disease that even all the antibiotics in the world can't cure."

AIRBORNE
TRANSMITTED
DISEASES

CHAPTER 9

'There are only two things that children
spontaneously give others: their contagious
diseases and the age of their mother.'
—Benjamin Spock

Suffering from Consumption

The cough would not cease. At night, Sam began having fever, chills and drenched his bed sheets with sweat. His appetite was good, but he kept losing weight. Then one day, he started coughing up blood. The village doctor examined Sam and told him that he was most likely suffering from consumption or wasting disease. These terms were not familiar to Sam, so he asked the doctor to elaborate, "I am afraid that you may have tuberculosis," the doctor explained. "Furthermore, I recommended that you take the next bus into the city and get a chest X-ray."

—A peace corps worker living in Central Africa

TUBERCULOSIS

Tuberculosis (TB) has a worldwide distribution but is endemic in impoverished countries. Lately, however, with the increasing prevalence of AIDS and influx of immigrants, the incidence of tuberculosis in the United States and other developed countries is on the rise. The most common mode of tuberculous transmission is by inhalation of infected droplets from the cough of an infected person. A less common form of transmission is by drinking unpasteurised milk or milk products. Overcrowding and poverty promote the dissemination of tuberculosis.

Most countries where tuberculosis is endemic recommend or require BCG vaccination. The vaccine is safe; however, its efficiency has been in question. Although the degree of protection against tuberculosis is uncertain, the vaccine does appear to limit the severity of the disease. In the United States, BCG vaccination is not ordinarily given, since the incidence of tuberculosis has been low. Therefore early detection and treatment has been the major means of preventing outbreaks of this disease. However, BCG vaccination may be justified for those planning to live or do extensive long-term travel in highly endemic areas.

Alternately, a tuberculin skin test can be done before departure and repeated after returning from an endemic area. If the return tuberculin test becomes positive, treatment with anti-tuberculosis medication is indicated. Furthermore, anyone who has never received BCG vaccination but has a positive tuberculosis test should consult their doctor concerning treatment.

MENINGOCOCCAL

Meningococcal disease is spread from person to person through inhalation of infected droplets (such as from coughing or sneezing). Meningococcal disease can result in a deadly blood infection (septicaemia) or meningitis.

Epidemics occur during the dry season (December through June) in sub-Saharan Africa. They are particularly common in the so-called 'meningitis belt' of the savannah areas extending from Mali eastward to Ethiopia.

Recent epidemics have also occurred in Kenya, Tanzania and Nepal. Although travellers to these areas rarely contract meningococcal disease, the vaccination is recommended in view of its deadly consequences.

The vaccine is given as a single subcutaneous injection.

Saudi Arabia requires for all pilgrims of the hajj to Mecca to be vaccinated.

POLIO

Whether travelling or not, everyone should receive a primary series of vaccination against polio. Most developed countries routinely administer this primary series of vaccinations during infancy and childhood. There are two types of vaccine:

- the oral polio vaccine (OPV) which is composed of live, attenuated viruses
- inactivated polio vaccine (IPV) which is given by injection

Please see section on immunisation concerning vaccination recommendations.

SMALLPOX

One of the greatest medical achievements of this past century has been the successful eradication of smallpox. Smallpox was first reported in China during the first century AD and in Europe and Africa 700 AD. It was introduced into the Americas during the era of European colonisation during the 16th and 17th centuries where it devastated large populations of the indigenous inhabitants. The last reported natural occurring case of smallpox occurred in Somalia in October 1977. The last known case occurred one year later in September 1978 in Birmingham, England, as a result of a laboratory accident.

Since January 1982, smallpox has been deleted from the World Health Organisation International Health Regulations and vaccination is no longer indicated.

EIGHTH TRAVEL STORY

Little Tommy was a six-year-old Canadian boy who lived in Caracas, Venezuela. His father was employed by a major international oil firm and they had been residing in Venezuela for the past two years.

Tommy was enrolled at the International School. He was an only child and in addition to his parents, was cared for by a nanny. The parents were not only meticulous with his schooling but also with his medical care. During his routine medical check-ups, they made sure he was also up-to-date with his vaccinations. However, his parents were alarmed when they were told that his skin screening test (Tine test) for tuberculosis was positive. "Our son with tuberculosis, how can this be possible?," his father said.

Tommy's paediatrician took a meticulous medical history. In particular, he wanted to know all of Tommy's close personal contacts. Except for his schoolmates, Tommy's only close contacts were his parents and his nanny. On further questioning, the parents related that Tommy's nanny had been coughing lately, but they thought nothing of it. She had been with them for over a year and appeared to be healthy, although they could not recall her ever being seen by a doctor. On the doctor's advice, the nanny was brought to his office for an evaluation. Her general appearance was normal. However, on closer examination, she was noted to have abnormal crepitating sounds of her left upper chest. A chest X-ray was ordered which demonstrated a left upper lung infiltrate suspicious of tuberculosis. She had a productive cough. Therefore, sputum samples were analysed which confirmed the diagnosis of pulmonary tuberculosis. A chest X-ray was also done on Tommy and both his parents. Fortunately, all three of their chest X-rays were negative for pulmonary tuberculosis. Furthermore, skin testing of the parents for tuberculosis was negative. Apparently, Tommy had been exposed to the tuberculosis bacteria, but the disease was dormant.

Both Tommy and his nanny were started on medication for treatment of tuberculosis. Since his nanny had evidence of active tuberculosis, she needed to take more than one anti-tuberculous drug. The doctor reassured the parents that after a few days of taking the anti-tuberculosis drugs, the nanny would no longer be infectious to others. As such, there was no need to discontinue her employment as long as she took her medications as prescribed. Furthermore, her general physical examination did not reveal the presence of any other medical disorder to be of concern. Both Tommy and his nanny were told to take the medications for at least six months.

Tommy's parents were greatly relieved by the doctor's comments. However, in the future, they would make sure that any live-in nanny or domestic servant will have a medical check-up and a chest X-ray prior to commencement of duties. Since the family was also responsible for the general health and welfare or their domestic help, they would also arrange for annual medical check-ups, as well as keeping their vaccinations up-to-date.

There is one final lesson to be learned from Tommy's misfortune. When living abroad where tuberculosis is endemic, it is advisable to have a screening skin test for tuberculosis as part of the annual medical check-up. Early treatment of tuberculosis will prevent complications and chronic disability.

EMERGING DISEASES
SARS

In 2003 there was an outbreak of SARS that spread to over two dozen countries in Asia, North American, South America and Europe. According to the WHO, over 8,000 people worldwide became ill and 780 died before the epidemic was contained. At this time there are no reported cases of SARS, but many authorities feel it is only a matter of time before it returns.

Severe acute respiratory syndrome (SARS) is a severe respiratory illness that is caused by a coronavirus.

Initially SARS begins with a fever greater than 100.4°F (38.0°C). Other early symptoms include headache, body aches, fatigue and mild respiratory complaints. Then, after two to seven days, SARS patients develop a dry cough and breathing problems.

SARS is spread primarily by direct person-to-person contact. In particular, touching infectious droplets or secretions of another person (such as on their skin or contaminated objects) and then touching your nose, eyes or mouth. This can happen if someone infected with SARS coughs or sneezes on others or nearby surfaces.

There is no vaccine against SARS, and the treatment of SARS is somewhat limited. Therefore, prevention is paramount. Here are some recommendations:

There is no telling if a SARS outbreak will recur. If one does, it is prudent to postpone elective or non-essential travel to those areas having an epidemic. The WHO and CDC organisations frequently issue and update travel alerts where epidemics are in progress. If a SARS outbreak occurs, avoid close contact with large numbers of people to minimise the risk of infection. Also wash hands after contact with other people or when using public facilities. The CDC does not recommend routine use of mask or protective equipment in public areas. However, a mask (N 95 or similar type) is recommended if you plan to visit a hospital (or clinic) that may be treating SARS patients or if you are in a high-risk occupation (hospital-based employees).

Above all else, if you develop a high fever, body aches, respiratory complaints or any other ill-defined symptoms, see your doctor. Your doctor can evaluate your condition, and if necessary, issue a letter attesting to your fitness and safety for flying.

Travellers should check with the CDC or WHO websites if SARS or any other epidemic is in progress at their planned destination. Another source of information is the regional health authority

Bird Flu

Avian Influenza (commonly known as Avian or bird flu) is a highly contagious disease affecting wild and domestic birds. The disease is caused by the H5NI virus (a sub-type of influenza A). Infected birds shed the virus in their secretions and droppings. The virus was first isolated in birds (terns) in South Africa in 1961. The disease is contagious and highly virulent to poultry. Fortunately, at this time the virus has a low propensity to infect humans. Infection in humans primarily occurs in bird handlers and close contact with infected poultry (infected chickens, ducks and turkeys). Transmission occurs by direct contact with infected birds or surfaces contaminated with excretions from infected birds. However, the mode of transmission of this disease to humans is still being investigated. All influenza virus are characterised by their ability to mutate into more virulent and transmittable strains. The overwhelming public health fear is that the H5N1 virus will mutate into a virulent form that readily spreads from person to person. The first case of direct birds to human transmission was documented in 1997 in Hong Kong during an epidemic of Avian Influenza in poultry. Since then, WHO has reported human cases of Avian Influenza in Asia, Africa, the Pacific, Europe and the Near East. Indonesia has reported the most cases.

Although H5N1 virus transmission to humans is rare, illness can be severe. The overall death rate approaches 60 per cent. The symptoms of Avian flu are similar to other influenza virus infections in humans and consist of fever, cough, sore throat, muscle aches. Progression of the disease leads to pneumonia, severe respiratory distress and death.

Outbreaks of Avian Influenza have been reported in China, Cambodia, Hong Kong, Indonesia, Japan, Laos, South Korea, Thailand and Vietnam. A few cases of people dying from it have been reported in Vietnam and Thailand. At that time, the virus caused a severe respiratory infection in 18 people (six of who died). Since then, there have been other cases of people getting Avian. There has been only a few cases of human-to-human transmission of the Avian influenza virus, since this mode of transmission is neither efficient nor sustainable.

Swine Flu

Influenza viruses are small RNA viruses that commonly infect mammals and birds. Swine flu is a respiratory infection of pigs caused by the type A influenza virus. Rarely does the virus infect humans. Prior transmissions have been limited, and seldom involving more than three people. However,in late March and early April 2009, a new variant of the Swine Influenza A (H1N1) was reported in Southern California, San Antonio and in Mexico. The new virus has genetic segments of swine from North America, Europe, and Asia, avian influenza viruses from North America, and human influenza viruses.

The influenza A (H1N1) virus is spread by sneezing or coughing like most flu viruses do. The virus can survive outside the body for two hours or longer. Therefore, it can also spread by touching contaminated surfaces such as doorknobs, tables and desk, and then touching the nose, eyes or mouth. There is no evidence that the virus spreads through the eating of pork products that have been thoroughly cooked.

The symptoms of Swine Flu are similar to most types of flu, consisting of fever, cough and sore throat. Frequently, muscle aches, fatigue and headache also occur. Some patients also have nausea, vomiting and diarrhea. Severely affected persons can develop pneumonia, respiratory failure and death. The swine flu is presumed to be contagious up to seven days after symptoms begin, or at least 24 hours after symptoms resolve, (whichever is longer). However, young children may be contagious for a longer period of time.

What Can Be Done to Avoid Bird or Swine Flu?

Measures that should be taken before travel:

- Assemble a travel kit containing first aid and medical supplies. It is important to include a thermometer and an alcohol-based disinfectant hand rub for hand hygiene.
- If possible, identify beforehand those countries that are experiencing an epidemic. It would be prudent to know of regional healthcare resources in case of sudden illness.
- Be sure that you are up to date on your flu and other immunisations.

Precautions While Travelling in an Endemic Area or During a Pandemic (Disease That Has Spread to a Large Area or Multiple Countries)

Avoid poultry farms, contact with animals in live food markets and any surfaces that appear to be contaminated with feces from poultry or other animals.

Practice frequent and appropriate hand hygiene. Clean your hands often with either soap and water or a waterless alcohol-base disinfectant hand rub to help prevent disease transmission. Always cover your mouth with a tissue or your hand when coughing. Reduce non-essential travel and visits to crowded public places during the pandemic. Maintain good immunity and resistance by drinking plenty of fluids, getting adequate sleep, having a healthy diet, and not smoking.

Above all, be concerned, but don't panic. As pandemics evolve, it is prudent to keep in touch with the local health authorities, the Center of Disease Control website (http://www.cdc.gov) and your doctor.

All foods from poultry (including eggs) should be thoroughly cooked. Influenza viruses are destroyed by heat.

If you developed respiratory symptoms or other illness, seek prompt medical attention. There are antiviral medications to help treat this illness. Many embassies have a list of reputable health care providers in the region.

Finally, after your return, monitor your health for ten days. If you developed any illness, contact your doctor and inform him/her of your recent travel itinerary.

VENOMOUS STINGS
AND BITES

CHAPTER 10

'You (the snake) will crawl on your belly
and eat dust all the days of your life.
And I will put enmity between you and the women,
and between your offspring and hers;
he will crush your head, and you will strike his heel.'
—Genesis 3:14-15

Beware the Black Widow Spider

George felt a sudden sting of his left big toe after putting on his shoes. He quickly removed his left shoe and out dropped a black spider about the size of a quarter. Within a few minutes, his left foot became swollen and red, and he had difficulty breathing. His wife called for an ambulance and he was admitted to the hospital.

—A camper in southern Arizona who was bitten by a black widow spider

SNAKE BITES

Contact with snakes and other venomous creatures is becoming more frequent as a result of greater access to remote areas and increasing popularity of outdoor recreation. Venomous creatures are found in terrestrial, aquatic and marine environments.

Venom is a complex mixture of proteins. The harmful effects of venom are the result of two separate actions, toxicity (poisoning) or anaphylaxis (allergic reaction). The first action, toxicity, can be subdivided depending on the body organ most affected. Types of toxicity include: neurotoxins (nervous system injury), hemolysin toxin (blood cell destruction), cardiotoxin (irregular heart rhythm or cardiac arrest), or proteolytic toxin (muscle and soft tissue damage).

The most notorious venomous creatures are the snakes which are distributed in the temperate and tropical habitats throughout the world. However fewer than 20 per cent of the nearly 2,700 species of snakes are venomous. Poisonous snakes can be divided into five separate families:

- The Elapidoe (cobras, kraits, mambas and coral snakes) which are found in all parts of the world except Europe. They are particularly prevalent in Australia.
- The Viperivae (or 'true vipers' including the adders) found in all parts of the world except America.
- The Hydrophidae (or sea snakes). They inhabit the tropical waters from the Persian Gulf to the southwest Pacific Ocean. Sea snakes are particularly abundant in the Indian Ocean and the Bay of Bengal.
- The Crotalidae (or pit vipers) found in Asia and America.
- The Colubridae (boomslangs, bird snakes) the largest family of snakes which are found throughout the world except Australia.

Please see the map showing the distribution of poisonous snakes in Southeast Asia. It has been estimated that over 300,000 poisonous snake bites worldwide occur every year, of which about 30,000 to 40,000 are fatal. The greatest number of these bites occur in Southeast Asia and the most frequent culprit is the cobra.

What are the Symptoms of a Venomous Snake Bite?

Initially, there is pain and swelling at the wound site. This is soon followed by bruises, discoloration and blisters and proximal lymph gland enlargement. Other adverse effects include low blood pressure, abnormal heart rhythms, kidney malfunction and bleeding disorders. Subsequently, breathing difficulties, convulsions, shock, coma and ultimately death can occur.

How to Prevent Snake Bites?

Snakes are usually not aggressive animals. They are shy of people and will not bite unless disturbed, stepped on or cornered. Snakes do not have ear openings or eardrums. They do have a hearing apparatus called an inner ear which is very sensitive to ground vibrations. However, they have a keen sense of smell and are very sensitive to ground vibrations such as approaching feet. Most snakes also have well-developed eyesight. Since most bites occur on the legs, the best prevention is to look where you are stepping and to wear high leather boots and long pants. If working with your hands, it is advisable to wear gloves.

What Should You Do if Bitten by a Snake?

Initially, an assessment should be made as to whether or not the snake is poisonous. A basic knowledge of indigenous snakes would be helpful. Also, if possible, the snake should be captured and killed for identification purpose. The size of the snake should be noted since larger snakes inflict greater quantities of venom. The wounds of venomous snakes are usually characterised by two fang punctures. Absence of fang wounds and symptoms within 20 minutes are strong evidence against a venomous bite.

If a venomous snake bite is suspected, the victim should be placed at rest, since running or excessive physical activities enhance distribution of the poison to the rest of the body. The extremity can be splinted to reduce mobility. Immediately, contact emergency medical services for transfer to a medical facility where advance medical treatment and anti-venom vaccine can be administered. If available, an Extractor Snake Bite Kit may be effective if used quickly. The extractor device works by applying a strong negative pressure to the bite wound to suck out some of the venom. This device has also been used for bites and stings of venomous insects, spiders, scorpions, and marine life. Incising puncture wounds, applying tourniquets, applying ice, or sucking out the venom by mouth is no longer recommended. All bite wounds should be covered with a dry, clean bandage.

INSECT STINGS AND BITES

Venomous insect stings and bites usually cause allergic reactions. These allergic reactions can range from localised swelling, pain, itching and hives to severe generalised reactions such as, breathing difficulties (bronchospasm), shock (anaphylaxis) and even death.

There are three major groups of venomous insects:

- The Apidae (bees)
- The Vespidae (wasp, hornets and yellow jackets)
- The Solenopsis (fire or red ants).

Treatment

Localised skin reactions can be treated with cool compresses, calamine lotion or anti-itching creams. It is important to inspect the wound carefully for stingers. If found, they should be removed gently as to not disrupt venom sacks which are sometimes attached. A needle or pen knife can be used to gently tease the stinger out, or a piece of plastic (such as a credit card) can be used to scrape the stinger. Do not use tweezers or finger tips. Generalised reactions such as hives can be treated with oral antihistamine medication. Acetaminophen, paracetamol, or ibuprofen may be taken for pain relief. However, more severe generalised reactions such as wheezing, breathing difficulties, swelling of the face and around the eyes and dizziness require urgent medical treatment. A self-administered epinephrine injection kit is advised for those with a history of severe allergic reactions to stings and insect bites. Following an injection, transfer to the nearest medical facility is still necessary, since the allergic reaction often returns as the epinephrine wears off.

Individuals who have a history of severe reactions to insect stings should consider carrying a syringe of epinephrine (adrenaline) when participating in outdoor activities. Commercial bee-sting kits are available which contain a syringe pre-loaded with adrenaline for immediate use and antihistamine tablets.

Prevention of insect bites and stings include wearing long pants when outdoors and avoid walking barefooted. Immunotherapy (or desensitisation) injections are recommended for those with a history of severe reactions to insect bites such as bees.

SCORPIONS, CENTIPEDES AND SPIDERS

These are members of the arachnid family that are capable of venomous bites and stings. There are at least 650 known species of scorpions and their habitats vary from tropical to arid. Although painful, scorpion stings of healthy adults are rarely fatal except for the stings of Androctonus australis of the Sahara and several Mexican species. However, stings of the very young and the elderly can sometimes be fatal.

Most spiders are not poisonous to human. In the United States, venomous spider bites are primarily associated with the black widow spider or the brown recluse spider.

The painful bite of a black widow spider is followed by muscle cramping, abdominal pain, sweating, nausea, headache and difficulty breathing. Although seldom is the bite fatal in healthy adults, it can be for young children and the elderly. Urgent medical treatment is necessary, and all children less than 16 years of age should be admitted to a hospital and given antivenim injections. Additional treatment includes muscle relaxants and analgesics including morphine.

Treatment for scorpions, centipedes and other spider bites is similar as that to venomous insect stings.

SOIL AND WATER-BORNE DISEASES

CHAPTER 11

'Do not walk barefoot'
—Advice from a guide at a
coffee plantation in South America

Most of the human population is or has been infected with parasites. Parasites are endemic throughout the world and have probably caused illnesses since the beginning of the human race. Recent autopsies of Egyptian mummies have testified to the diversity and prevalence of parasitic infections since ancient times. The mechanism by which parasites invade humans vary. Parasites such as Necator/Ancylostoma (hookworm) and schistosomiasis burrow into the skin. Some such as pneumocystis are inhaled. Others such as malaria, filariasis, babesiosis, chagas disease or African trypanosomiasis (or African sleeping sickness) are transmitted by mosquitoes or blood-sucking insects. Trichomomoniasis is a venereal infection. However, the greatest number of parasites are transmitted by contaminated food and water (amoeba, giardia, intestinal nematodes [worms]).

Measures to avoid contracting parasitic infections such as food and drink precautions, ways to prevent mosquito and insect bites and protection against venereal diseases have been previously elaborated on. What has not been discussed are the health hazards associated with soil and water-borne diseases.

SCHISTOSOMIASIS

Travellers should avoid swimming in stagnant or slow-moving fresh water in the tropics, as there is a risk of contracting schistosomiasis. This disease is prevalent in parts of South

America (Brazil, Venezuela and Surinam), some Caribbean islands, Africa, the Middle East and the Far East (mostly China, Philippines, Thailand, Laos and Cambodia). It is estimated that as many as 200 million people may be infected worldwide. Humans become infected after contact with water infested with the infective stage of the parasite. The parasite burrows into the skin causing intense local itching and irritation. Then, in about two to six weeks after exposure, generalised symptoms such as fever, chills, headache, hives, abdominal pain, diarrhoea, cough and generalised weakness may occur. These symptoms gradually subside but may last as long as two to three months.

However, if the parasites have not been detected and treated, long-term detrimental effects to the liver, kidneys and urinary tract may occur.

Since there is no way of telling if the water is infested, it is best to avoid swimming, wading or drinking any fresh water in endemic countries. Since the flukes' life span is seldom longer than 48 hours, storing water for three days will make it safe for bathing. If inadvertent exposure to infested water occurs, immediate vigorous drying with a towel followed by application of rubbing alcohol to the exposed skin area may lessen the risk of infection. Anyone who thinks he has been exposed to the disease should consult a physician for blood, urine and stool testing. Effective treatment is available but best started early in order to avoid long-term sequel.

HOOKWORM DISEASE, STRONGYLOIDIASIS AND CUTANEOUS LARVA MIGRANS

Travellers should also avoid walking barefoot in the tropics, especially near villages or beaches where sanitation measures are lacking. In these areas, hookworm (Ancylostoma/Necator) may be endemic. It is estimated that over 900 million people worldwide are infected. The eggs of the parasite are deposited in the soil after human defecation. After a couple of days, the eggs hatched into infective larvae that remain viable in the soil for several weeks. They burrow into exposed skin (usually the feet) resulting in localised itching, redness and swelling ('ground itch'). They then migrate from the skin, into the blood, lungs, then ultimately mature in the intestines where they feed on blood. In large numbers, they can cause severe anaemia, growth retardation, shortness of breath and generalised weakness. Treatment is usually with either pyrantel pamoate or mebendazole.

Other skin-burrowing parasites in tropical soils include strongyloidiasis and cutaneous larva migrans (creeping eruption).

The best means of protection against these parasites is by wearing shoes when walking in endemic areas and avoiding direct skin to soil contact.

MELIOIDOSIS

Melioidosis is a mysterious, tropical soil disease of humans and animals caused by the bacteria Pseudomonas pseudomallei. The disease has been reported throughout the tropics, but is endemic primarily in Southeast Asia. The bacteria is a saprophyte which grows in wet soil, ponds and rice paddies. The disease was first described by a British pathologist working in Burma in 1911. For many years, it was dismissed as an uncommon illness, until hundreds of American soldiers became very ill from it during the Vietnam war. The rural poor are most likely to be exposed to melioidosis as a result of their close contact with soil and water. Since they are the least likely to have access to sophisticated medical care, it is probable that active clinical melioidosis is under diagnosed in many countries.

Melioidosis is primarily contracted by soil contamination of skin wounds and abrasions. Less common routes include ingestion and inhalation. The disease is not thought to be contagious and person to person transmission is rare. The symptoms of the disease are variable and can mimic many other illness. Often, the disease is not recognised until the victim is critically ill. Lung infection is the most common presentation. However, the disease may occur in the blood (septicaemia), as well as many organs including the skin, brain, lungs, heart, liver, bones, joints and even the eyes. Victims can also have insidious or dormant infections that only become symptomatic many years from the time of exposure. Even today, Vietnam American veterans continue to succumb to the disease.

Diagnosis of the infection is usually made by laboratory culture of the organism. Antibody levels can be measured in blood test. However, this test is only helpful to research the incidence of the disease for a particular region.

Melioidosis is resistant to many antibiotics. Milder forms of the disease such as those involving the skin can be drained or surgically excised. However, relapse of the infection, even years later is frequent. Severe cases such as those involving the lungs or blood (septicaemia) are often fatal.

There is no vaccine against melioidosis. Therefore, wounds and abrasions that are contaminated by soil in endemic regions should be thoroughly cleaned and washed with soap and water. After which, an antiseptic cream should be applied and the wound bandaged. All deep or infected wounds should be treated by a doctor.

NINTH TRAVEL STORY

Mark's father worked at the consular section of the Canadian Embassy in Cairo. He was on a three-year assignment in Egypt. Mark was 16 years old and attended the International School. Cairo was a fascinating city, rich in Middle Eastern culture, religion and of course, steeped in archaeology. Besides the renowned Sphinx and pyramids, there were many ancient Coptic churches, mosques and Egyptian temples of antiquity. The school organised many educational trips to these sites. Mark even got a chance to sail on a felucca, a small sailing vessel similar to those used during the reign of the pharaohs.

Cairo was also a scorching hot, polluted and congested city. On several occasions, to escape the intense heat, Mark and several of his school mates would travel to the outskirts of the city and go swimming in the freshwater canals. A complex canal network linked the irrigation plains to the Nile River. Although Mark was careful not to drink tap or unbottled water in Cairo, he did not consider swimming to be a health hazard.

After his swims, he sometimes developed itching of his arms and legs, but thought nothing of it. Then a few weeks later, he developed a fever associated with muscle aches, headache and cough. The parents brought Mark to the embassy's physician who prescribed analgesics and cough syrups for what was thought to be a flu. However, a couple of days later, he developed hives, abdominal pains and diarrhoea. Mark was brought back to the doctor. A blood test was done which demonstrated an increase number of eosinophils cells in his blood. These cells often proliferate in response to parasitic infections. Therefore stool analysis was done, and Mark was found to be shedding numerous schistosome eggs. An antibody blood test for schistosomiasis was also reported to be positive.

Mark was treated with a medication named praziquantel. After a couple of days, his symptoms subsided and he was able to return to school. Never again would he swim in freshwater within the Nile Valley.

Schistosomiasis is endemic throughout the Nile Valley and its delta. The infection can easily be prevented by not bathing or swimming in waters likely to be infested with the snail host of this parasite. In endemic areas like Egypt, only water that has been chlorinated, such as swimming pools, can be considered safe. Don't fall victim to 'the curse of the Nile'.

RABIES

CHAPTER 12

'Beware of the Dog.'
—Petronius, AD 1st century

Don't Feed the Monkeys!

While exploring the Southern Indian temple, Cindy couldn't resist feeding the monkeys. However, while talking to her friend, a monkey came from behind her and bit the hand which was holding a piece of bread. Cindy screamed in agony and her face contorted in pain as she felt the primates teeth pierce her skin. She rushed back to her hotel, where she cleaned the puncture wound with soap and water. She then applied a disinfectant solution and antibiotic cream. However, later that evening, the wound began to fester and she developed a fever. The glands beneath her arm also became swollen and painful. She visited a local doctor who recommended admission to a hospital for intravenous antibiotics. However, Cindy was shocked when the doctor told her that she might contract rabies. Worse yet, the vaccine was not locally available!

—A traveller visiting temples in southern India

Monkey business aside, Cindy's life is in mortal danger. She needs to be vaccinated against rabies and soon. Since, once symptoms begin, the disease is invariably fatal.

Rabies is a disease endemic to many countries in Central and Southeast Asia (but not Singapore), Africa, the Indian subcontinent and tropical Central and South America. With increasing numbers of travellers to these regions, exposure to rabies is becoming a greater health risk.

WHAT IS RABIES?

Rabies is a disease of the nervous system caused by the deadly rhabdovirus. It is primarily transmitted by the infected saliva of animals. Infected (or rabid) animals are of two groups:

- the urban or domestic animals such as unimmunised dogs and cats
- the wild (sylvatic) animals such as skunks, foxes, racoons, mangooses, wolves, bats or monkeys.

In most areas of the world, the dog is the principle source of human infection.

SYMPTOMS

After being bitten by an infected animal, the incubation period of rabies may range from ten days to over one year (but the average time is one to two months). To a large extent, the incubation time depends on the amount of virus introduced and the location of the bite.

The first symptoms are non-specific and consist of fever, headaches, lethargy, muscle aches, nausea, vomiting, sore throat or mild cough. These symptoms last from one to four days. Subsequently, the patient develops confusion, excitability, agitation and abnormalities of the autonomic nervous system including dilated pupils, excessive sweating, salivation, difficulty in swallowing and a low blood pressure. Ultimately, the patient lapses into coma and dies of respiratory arrest.

PREVENTION

Once the symptoms of rabies begin, there is no effective treatment and death usually occurs within several days. Fortunately, the disease can be prevented by early wound treatment and administration of vaccines. All animal wounds should be immediately scrubbed with soap and then flushed with water. Tetanus toxoid injection and antibiotics should also be given. Animal bite wounds should not be sutured or closed.

If bitten by a wild or a stray domestic animal (especially if unprovoked or exhibiting unusual behaviour), the animal should be captured and destroyed. Its brain should then be sent for laboratory analysis. If rabies is confirmed or the animal cannot be captured, then immunisation needs to be given. Immunisation consists of intramuscular injections of both:

- rabies immune globulin (for immediate but short-lasting protection against rabies)
- rabies vaccine (for development of lasting protection)

If bitten by a healthy dog or cat in an area endemic for rabies, it should be captured and closely observed for ten days. If the animal exhibits any illness or abnormal behaviour during this period, it should be killed and its brain analysed for rabies infection. If the brain analysis is negative, no vaccination is necessary.

For those individuals who have greater exposure to rabies, such as veterinarians, cave explorers, animal handlers or workers in endemic areas, pre-exposure vaccination is recommended to strengthen their immunity against this virus. This involves giving three vaccinations over the course of one month.

TENTH TRAVEL STORY

Father John, a Canadian, was the headmaster of a Catholic missionary school in Patna, India. He had been posted to the subcontinent eight years ago, and under his guidance, the school had grown from a mere handful of students to over 300 at latest count. He was also active within the small Catholic community, arranging assistance for the needy and providing spiritual support. Patna was a congested city teeming with humanity. The air was thick and hazy from traffic pollution. Open sewage gutters parallel many of the side streets. The public amenities were unable to keep up with the unrelenting population growth.

Cows, considered sacred by the Hindus, were allowed to roam freely within the city, often holding up traffic and disturbing the local hawkers. The greatest menace of all, however, were the packs of roaming dogs.

One evening, while Father John was walking down a back alley, a black, mangy and scrawny dog suddenly appeared and without provocation, bit him on the lower left leg. The wound had just barely broke the skin. Father John washed it, applied mercurochrome and then plaster. Since it was such a minor injury, he did not think medical attention was necessary, and sure enough, the wound healed completely within a few days. The whole incident was soon forgotten.

Weeks passed and Father John proceeded with his work and numerous commitments. However, one morning, he developed a flu-like illness associated with muscle aches, headache, nausea, malaise and fever. His appetite was poor, he had a dry cough and his throat became painful. He also developed twitching and spasm of the muscles of his lower left leg. Father John stayed in bed during the next two days and took paracetamol tablets for his fever and muscle aches. However, by the third day, he felt worse and a doctor was summoned to see him. His behaviour had changed. Father John had now become agitated, excitable and even combative. At times, he was confused and began having hallucinations. Father John was admitted to the Patna General Hospital for evaluation. During his first day there, he developed involuntary contractions of his arms and legs. His pupils became dilated and he developed excessive eye tearing, salivation and sweating. His mental state would fluctuate between lucid and irrational intervals.

In view of the progressive deterioration of his mental and neurologic function, a tentative diagnosis of rabies was made. Father John was unable to swallow and needed to be hydrated with an intravenous drip. The school and Catholic community became greatly alarmed over the sudden illness that had befallen on their priest. Anti-rabies vaccination was recommended, although the doctors stated that its effectiveness was limited at this stage of his illness. Since it was not available in Patna, arrangements were made to evacuate him to the nearest centre of medical expertise, which was Bangkok.

The patient arrived there safely and was immediately admitted to the intensive care unit of the Bangkok General Hospital. The hospital staff were very careful in handling all body fluids and secretions from the patient. Despite the precautions, one doctor was greatly alarmed when the priest involuntarily spat on him. Father John's respiration became erratic and he lapsed into a stupor. There was no choice but to place him on a respirator. However, he progressively became deeply comatose and on the following day expired.

The news of the priest's demise greatly sadden the teachers and the Catholic community in Patna. Services were held in his honour and tribute paid by the community elders. Within a month, the Catholic archdiocese sent a new headmaster to the school. A plaque was erected at the entrance of the school's gate in memory of the contributions of the late Father John. The new headmaster had been pre-vaccinated with anti-rabies serum prior to his arrival in India.

The most tragic aspect of this story is that Father John's demise could have been prevented. Anti-rabies vaccination, if started early after a suspected rabies bite, is very effective. The vaccine is given by a series of injections (initially, then at 3, 7, 14, 21, 28 and 90 days later). Alternatively, anti-rabies vaccinations can be given pre-exposure for those planning to live in endemic areas. Therefore if subsequently bitten by a suspected rabid animal, only two booster injections of the vaccine are all that is necessary. Once symptoms have began, there is no effective treatment! Therefore, prevention while visiting endemic regions is paramount. Preventative measures include avoiding areas where stray dogs roam, and avoid feeding or touching wild animals such as monkeys.

COMMON SKIN PROBLEMS

CHAPTER 13

'There's a fungus, among us.'
—Anonymous

A Terrible Itch

A few weeks after arriving in the tropics, Jane developed an itchy rash under her arms, beneath her breasts and in the groin. She applied a hydrocortisone cream which she took from her medical kit, but after a few days, the rash only became worse. Jane saw a doctor who did a skin scraping of the rash and under the microscope, determined that she had a disseminated fungal infection. She was treated with antifungal tablets and creams for a couple of weeks, and the rash disappeared. She was also given instructions to help prevent a recurrence.

—A lady prone to fungal infections in the tropics

HEAT RASH

Heat rash (also known as prickly rash or miliaria) most commonly develops in skin folds and wherever clothing causes friction. Infants commonly develop the rash on the head, neck, shoulders, chest and back, groin and armpits. Symptoms range from superficial blisters to red bumps. Sometimes the rash can be intensely itchy or prickly. Heat rash occurs when sweat glands in the skin become blocked. Then instead of evaporating, the perspiration remains trapped beneath the skin causing inflammation and rash. This disorder occurs most frequently in those visiting the tropics. Acclimation occurs over months, during which the problem usually resolves. Intense physical activity and excessive sweating intensifies the rash. Occasionally, heat rash can become infected with bacteria, resulting in pustules. Prevention is by wearing soft, lightweight loose cotton clothing, and when possible staying in shaded, well-ventilated places. Usually this rash will resolve on its own. However, bathing in cool water and using non-drying soaps can help. Itchy skin can be soothed with calamine lotion. However, avoid using powders, creams or ointments which can further block skin pores and exacerbate the problem.

FUNGAL INFECTIONS

The heat and humidity can cause skin infections not normally a problem in cooler climates. Foremost among them are fungal skin infections, medically known as dermatophytosis.

The site of infection will vary according to the type of fungus involved.

Foot infection (commonly known as athlete's foot but also called 'Hong Kong Foot' by many Chinese) is caused by the fungus Tinea pedis. Symptoms include fissuring, itching and scaling of the toe webs and soles of the feet. As a result of breaks in the skin, secondary bacterial infections (cellulitis) can occur. Infections of the hand are similar but much less common than foot involvement.

Fungus also commonly infects the toenails (and sometimes finger nails) a condition called onychomycosis. The nails become discoloured, thickened, cracked and chalky.

Scalp infections (Tinea capitis) and beard (Tinea barbae) are characterised by patches of hair loss, scaling and itching. Skin infections of the trunk, arms and legs may be circumscribed in shape (ring worm) or appears as brown or white patches (Tinea versicolour).

Fungal infections can often be diagnosed by their characteristic appearance. However, some lesions must be scrapped and the fragments viewed under a microscope to confirm the diagnosis..

The best way to prevent fungal infections is by good hygiene and reducing excessive skin moisture. After bathing, carefully dry your feet (especially between the toes) and skin fold regions. Then apply a bland powder. If necessary, anti-fungal powders (e.g. miconazaole) may be used for greater protection. Wear loose-fitting cotton fabrics. It is also advisable to avoid sharing towels and washcloths.

Many fungal skin infections are easily treated with antifungal creams. However, extensive skin involvement as well as infection of the nails are best treated with oral medication such as itraconazole and terbinafine which requires a doctor's prescription. Recently, an antifungal nail lacquer (Loceryl) manufactured by Roche has become available for treatment of fungal nail infections. The active ingredient is amorolfine, and the lacquer should be applied to affected finger or toe nails once or twice weekly. It is safe and effective. However, it is relatively expensive and can only be obtained by prescription.

BACTERIAL SKIN INFECTIONS

Bacterial skin infections are also more common in the tropics and are often the result of excessive sweating, friction, or poor hygiene. Staphylococcus or Streptococcus bacteria are usually the cause of these infections. Infection frequently involve the hair and sweat glands (folliculitis), skin (cellulites) or lymph glands (lymphangitis). They also cause skin boils and slow healing 'tropical skin ulcers'.

Folliculitis can be treated with topical antibiotics and hot compresses. The other types of bacterial infection usually requires oral antibiotics. After treatment, 'decolonising' the skin by washing the entire body with an antiseptic soap containing either hexachlorophene, chlorhexidine or triclosan may prevent a recurrence. These soaps leave an inhibitory residue on the skin. Preventing relapses may also require elimination of nasal carriage of Staphylococcus. Applying mupirocin cream twice daily for five days each month may do this.

SKIN ALLERGIES

Manifestations of skin allergies include: 1) allergic contact dermatitis (itching, redness, occasionally blisters) as seen in poison ivy and exposure to nickel in costume jewelry 2) eczema and allergic dermatitis (itching, scales, and oozing blisters) or urticaria (red, itchy, raised bumps, 'hives'). There are many chemical and biologic substances that can cause skin allergies. In the tropics, allergies can occur after contact with certain tropical fruit, particularly mangoes. Mango belongs to the Anacardiaceae family, which includes cashew nuts, sumac, poison ivy and poison oak. The substance in mangoes that causes allergic skin rashes is urushiol, the oil in the poison ivy plant. When in season, mango is the most common plant-induced skin allergy in Hawaii. The rash is often limited to the angles of the mouth and cheeks. However, it can spread and affect other parts of the body. Occasionally papaya, pineapple and other citrus fruit can cause skin allergies. Certain tropical woods, particularly rosewood, can also cause skin allergies. Skin patch testing may be helpful when the cause of recurrent skin rash remains uncertain.

ACNE

Pimples is the layman's term for acne. Acne is most prevalent during adolescence. Although the cause of acne is unknown, it is thought to be secondary to inflammation and infection of the oil-secreting (sebaceous) glands. It occurs predominantly on the face and to a lesser extent on the back, chest and shoulders. These is no good evidence that particular foods alter the course or severity of acne. The face should be washed daily in order to remove excessive oil as well as bacteria on the skin surface. Mild acne can be treated by applying creams, lotions or gels that contain either benzoyl peroxide, retinoic acid or antibiotics. More complex cases often requires treatment with oral antibiotics (such as tetracycline) or isotretinoin (vitamin A derivatives). Your doctor or dermatologist will advise you accordingly.

DRY AND ROUGH SKIN

Travelling in cold, dry or windy environments may leave your skin as rough as a reptile. Dry and rough skin also commonly occurs during long plane journeys (where cabin air pressure and humidity are low) and staying in air-condition facilities. The elderly, in particular are prone to dry, flaking and rough skin.

What Can Be Done?

Always drink extra fluids. Apply skin emollients or oils regularly since they help retain skin moisture. Olive oil is not only considered as healthy in our diet, it also has beneficial effects when applied to dry and rough skin. Please see Chapter Two for additional advice concerning prevention and treatment.

DANDRUFF

Dandruff (seborrheic dermatitis) is characterised by greasy skin patches and flaking involving the scalp and eyebrows. It is thought to be caused by an inflammatory reaction to a type of yeast (Pityrosporum ovale). Dandruff can be treated with shampoos containing either zinc pyrithione, crude coal tar (Tegrin) or selenium sulfide (Selsun Blue). However, selenium sulfide can sometimes irritate the scalp and discolour the hair. Recently, a shampoo containing ketoconazole (Nizoral), an antifungal agent, has become available for difficult dandruff cases. However, it is relatively expensive and can only be sold by prescription.

LOUSE-BORNE INFECTIONS

Louse-borne infections (also known as pediculosis) are caused by small parasitic insects that cling to body hair and suck blood from their host. They are readily transferred to others by direct body contact, towels, discarded clothing, sharing combs and brushes, chair backs or infested bedding. There are three types of lice: 1) head lice (Pediculus capitis) 2) body lice (Pediculus corpus) and 3) crab lice (Phthirius pubis). Head lice infections occur in all socio-economic group, especially children. In contrast, body lice occur primarily in the poor and transient who are unable to maintain basic levels of personal hygiene. Crab lice inhabit the pubic hair regions, and are transmitted primarily by sexual activities. Their presence is often associated with other venereal infections. Diagnosis can be made by careful inspection (preferably with a magnifying glass) of hair for lice and their egg sacks (nits). Nits are shiny and smooth white specks that are firmly attached to hairs.

The primary symptom of all louse-borne infections is that of intense itching. Scratching can result in secondary skin irritation and infection. Effective treatment can be carried out by applying lotions containing either 1 per cent pyrethrin (Nix-approved for head lice only), piperonyl butoxide (RID), or lindane (1 per cent gamma benzine hexachloride, KWELL). These topical agents must be used as directed since excessive use can result in harmful side effects. Kwell should not be used on infants or pregnant mothers. After treatment, a fine comb can be used to remove lice and nits. A second treatment is usually recommended in one week's time, since the nits may be resistant to these agents and will hatch one week later. Combs and brushes should be heated in water to 65°C for five minutes or soaked in 25 Lysol. Clothing and bedding of an infected person should be washed in hot water. The scalps of family members should also be checked and treated as necessary.

Scabies are very small parasitic insects that actually burrow into the skin. Similar to lice, this is a cosmopolitan infection, and is commonly called the 'seven year itch'. Symptoms include intense itching, especially at night or after a hot bath. Dark wavy lines may appear in the skin, particularly in the arms, wrist and between the fingers. However, these lesions can appear anywhere on the body of those with severe infections or in babies. Often several members of a living group are infected. Treatment is by applying lotions or creams containing agents such as: 1) Lindane (gamma benzene hexachloride) 2) crotamiton (Eruax) or 3) benzyl benzoate (25 per cent). These agents are applied thinly, but should cover the entire body from the neck down. Lindane should be left on for eight to 12 hours. It should not be used during pregnancy or in babies. Bed linen, clothing and towels must be washed in hot water.

BEWARE OF THE SUN

CHAPTER 14

'Mad dogs and Englishmen go out in the midday sun.'
—Noel Coward

Watch the Sun!

It had been a great day at the beach. Clear blue water, overhanging palm trees, pristine white sand and plenty of glorious sunshine. As the sun's warmth waxed with sunset, the glow of Jack's body waned as the evening progressed. By midnight, he was in agony. His skin became as red as a boiled Maine lobster and excruciating to the touch. He was unable to sleep and felt feverish. The following day, the skin on his shoulders and back began to blister and ooze a sticky fluid.

—A weekend warrior oblivious to the harmful effects of the sun

Jack's misfortune is a classic example of too much of a good thing. Sunlight is an obvious source of comfort and enjoyment within our environment. Other beneficial effects of sunlight include warmth and vitamin D synthesis which promotes healthy bones and teeth.

The sun's energy encompasses a broad range from ultrashort ionising radiation to ultralong radiowaves of very low photon energy. However, the components of light that reaches earth's surface are narrow and primarily made up of ultraviolet (UV), visible light and infrared spectrum. The short UV rays known as ultraviolet B (UVB) are the ones that cause sunburn and can damage the genetic make-up (DNA) of skin cells. UVB rays are much stronger during the summer, at high altitudes and near the equator. UV rays are partially absorbed by stratospheric ozone. Concern about the destruction of ozone by chlorofluorocarbons released

into the atmosphere has led to international agreement to reduce production of these chemicals.

WHAT ARE THE ADVERSE EFFECTS OF SUNLIGHT?

The most common affliction resulting from excessive sun exposure is sunburn. Generally speaking, the ability of an individual to tolerate sunlight is inversely related to the amount of melanin skin pigmentation. In essence, the body puts up a shield against the sun by stimulating melanocytes to produce this pigment which darkens the skin and absorbs UV rays. Tolerance to sun exposure can usually be ascertained by asking an individual two questions:

- Do you always, sometimes, or never burn after sun exposure on unprotected skin?
- Do you never, sometimes, or always tan?

The answers to these questions will divide the population into six skin types varying from type I (always burn, never tan) to type VI (never burn, always tan).

The chronic effects of sun exposure can be divided into two groups—those related to accelerated ageing and those related to malignancy (cancer). With accelerated ageing, the skin rapidly loses its elasticity and develops a leathery texture.

In fact, much of what was originally considered as natural skin ageing is now attributed to sun exposure. This can be easily demonstrated by comparing the skin texture of the back of your hand with that of your inner arm which is seldom exposed to the sun. Ageing features of photodamaged sun-exposed skin include wrinkling, blotching and a roughened 'weather-beaten' appearance.

Malignant

Malignant features of photodamaged skin consist of skin growths (or tumours) and cancer. Initial skin growths that develop as a result of excessive sun exposure are harmless papillomas. The final step in the malignant process is the transformation of these skin growths into cancer. The three types of skin cancers associated with sun exposure are squamous cell carcinoma, basal cell carcinoma and melanoma, the latter being the most serious.

In addition to skin damage, there is also recent evidence to suggest that excessive exposure to solar radiation can diminish your body's immune defences.

PREVENTION
Stay Out of the Sun

This approach will minimise the harmful effects of ultraviolet rays. Unfortunately, social pressures make this an impractical solution for most individuals.

Protective Clothing

Clothing constructed of tightly woven fabrics, irrespective of colour, affords substantial protection. Partially transparent clothing such as T-shirts provide only minimal protection. As a general rule, if the clothing does not cast a dense shadow, then the protection is adequate. Also wear long sleeves and pants and a wide brimmed hat (not just a sun visor).

Sunscreens

Sunscreens are of two major types—chemical and physical. Chemical sunscreens absorb ultraviolet energy, thereby diminishing absorption by the skin. The major categories

of chemical sunscreens include p-aminobenzoic acid and its esters, benzophenones, anthranilates, cinnamates and salicylates. Physical sunscreens are light-opaque mixtures containing zinc oxide, talc or titanium oxide that scatter light, thereby reducing absorption by the skin.

Sunscreens are rated for their photoprotection effect by their 'sun protective factor' (SPF). The SPF is simply a ratio of the sun exposure time required to produce redness. The higher the SPF, the greater the protection. For example, if you turn pink after 10 minutes in the sun without protection, a SPF of 15 theoretically will give you 2.5 hours of protection (10 minutes x 15 = 150 minutes). SPF ratings of 15 or higher provide effective protection for most people against ultraviolet energy. However, fair skin individual should use a SPF of 25 or 30. After a SPF of 30, there is diminishing returns of sun protection as well as increased cost.

In addition to light absorption, another important aspect of sunscreens is their ability to stay on the skin, a property known as substantivity. The PABA esters formulated in moisturising vehicles provide the greatest substantivity, however, they may cause skin irritation for those with sensitive skin.

Limit Exposure

Photoprotection can also be achieved by limiting the time of exposure during the day. Since as much as half of an individual's total lifetime sun exposure may occur by the age of 18, it is essential to educate parents and their children about the hazards of excessive sunlight. Simply eliminating exposure at midday will substantially reduce the harmful effects of UV rays.

Medical Examination

Fortunately, skin cancer is easy to detect and when found early, even melanoma can be treated successfully. Many skin cancer foundations recommend doing a 10-minute full-body check every three months using a full length and hand mirror. Look for new skin discoloration or growths and any changes in the shape, size or colour of moles, birthmarks or freckles. If you notice anything unusual, be sure to see your regular doctor or a dermatologist as soon as possible.

HOW TO TREAT SUNBURN

Treat mild sunburn as you would any minor burn injury with cool compresses and analgesic sprays or ointments. If you sustain a severe sunburn (such as those falling asleep while in the sun), immediately take a cool bath or shower. Then apply a mild steroid cream such as hydrocortisone to all areas of the body involved. If blisters are formed, do not puncture them! If the blisters break on their own, gently remove the dead skin fragments with a sterile tweezers. Then apply an antibiotic cream and bandage with a clean dressing which will help protect the wound from infection.

Aspirin, ibuprofen or other non-steroid anti-inflammatory medication may be taken several times a day to relieve fever, pain and swelling. If allergic to these types of medications, then take either paracetamol or acetaminophen.

Make sure your tetanus vaccination is up-to-date. Severe cases of sun and heat exposure can result in high fever, chills, nausea and delirium. In these cases, a doctor should be consulted and possibly admission to a hospital.

HIGH ALTITUDE SICKNESS

CHAPTER 15

'Come down, O maid, from yonder mountain height:
What pleasure lives in height?'
—Lord Tennyson

Hit by High Altitude Sickness

While hiking on the Annapurna trail in Nepal at 12,000 feet, Tim became dizzy and complained of a headache. His feet became heavy and clumsy. After several minutes, the headache was so intense that he was unable to concentrate. He felt dizzy, sat down and suddenly began to vomit. He became disoriented and his speech was incoherent. Tim's hiking companions were alarmed by his rapid deterioration and immediately tried to carry him down the mountain.

—The effects of mountain sickness on a trekker in Nepal

Planning a trip to Nepal, or a hike in the Alps or Rockies? If so, have a great trip but beware of the dangers of high altitude sickness.

WHAT IS HIGH ALTITUDE SICKNESS?

High altitude sickness (also called acute mountain illness) often occurs when exerting oneself 8,000 feet above sea level. The incidence of side effects has been reported to range from 25 per cent at 7,000 feet to 50 per cent at 15,000 feet. It is more common in those who are young and physically fit, perhaps because they are the ones most physically active.

Although the cause of high altitude sickness is not completely understood, it appears to be related to a lack of oxygen (hypoxia).

Oxygen is an essential part of the metabolism and breakdown of sugar (glucose) into energy. In essence, the body is like an engine that uses oxygen as a source of fuel.

However, the higher the altitude, the less oxygen there is in the atmosphere. Consequently, like an engine running out of fuel, the body begins to hesitate, sputter and then stalls.

As oxygen becomes depleted with higher altitude, the body adapts by various physiologic mechanisms.

Blood vessels begin to dilate in order to bring more blood to the tissues. The heart rate increases, there is retention of fluids and breathing becomes more rapid (hyperventilation).

However, these compensatory mechanisms are limited and with progressive elevation complications begin. The lungs start retaining fluid (pulmonary edema) and the brain begins to swell (cerebral edema).

WHAT ARE THE SYMPTOMS OF ALTITUDE SICKNESS?

Initial symptoms of high altitude sickness are headaches, nausea, poor appetite, difficulty sleeping, cough, shortness of breath, muscle ache and generalised lethargy. These symptoms can occur anytime during ascent to high altitude but characteristically occur six to 48 hours later. As the illness progress, confusion and hallucinations occur, as well as a loss of concentration, coordination and judgement.

The late symptoms of high altitude sickness are stupor, coma, respiratory failure and ultimately death.

HOW CAN ALTITUDE SICKNESS BE TREATED?

The simplest and most effective treatment is to immediately descend to a lower altitude. This can easily be done while on a mountain climb. However, if you are on a plateau like in Tibet, this is not a practical solution.

Administration of oxygen will alleviate symptoms. It is also important to stay at rest until symptoms subside. Exertion of any kind will only exacerbate the condition. Medications such as aspirin, paracetamol, acetamenophen or ibufen can be taken to relieve headaches. Acetazolamide, especially if taken early, will help prevent or relieve cough and breathlessness. Steroids, such as dexamethasone, may help to reduce brain swelling. However, they may cause serious side effects and should be given only under the direction of a physician.

The symptoms and signs of mild high altitude sickness (such as cough, nausea and headache) usually subside within two to three days. However, any breathing difficulties or deterioration of mental function requires urgent medical treatment and evacuation.

HOW CAN ALTITUDE SICKNESS BE PREVENTED?

Physical conditioning at sea level will not prevent high altitude sickness. However, there are several ways to reduce the chances of becoming ill.

First, plan for a gradual ascent. During the initial two days, limit your climb to below the altitude of 8,000 feet. Sleeping at an altitude below 8,000 feet is especially important. On the subsequent days, limit your ascent to no more than 2,000 feet per day. If you are flying to a high altitude city such as La Paz, Boliva, plan to rest during the next couple of days. Do not engage in physical activities such as long walks, jogging or sporting activities.

What to Eat and Drink

A high carbonate diet may help reduce the symptoms of high altitude sickness. Avoid alcohol, sedatives and sleeping medications since they all depress respiration, lower oxygen intake and consequently increase the incidence of high altitude sickness.

Pre-treatment with acetazolamide (a mild diuretic) may prevent symptoms. It works by preventing fluid retention, increasing ventilation and increasing the oxygen saturation of blood.

Finally, if you have a cardiac or respiratory condition, it is advisable not to travel to high altitude destinations.

ELEVENTH TRAVEL STORY

Avoid getting too high when travelling. No, I am not talking about drug abuse. Every year, many travellers suffer adverse effects secondary to high altitude sickness, occasionally fatal.

If you are planning a trip to the Rockies, the Alps, Nepal or any other high altitude destination, be careful as to the pace of your ascent.

I myself have experienced the unpleasant effects of high altitude sickness during a visit to Tibet. However, my symptoms were very mild in comparison to my colleague Jeff, a young doctor who had recently finished his training in family medicine. What were we doing in Tibet? This is a question I even ask myself! It all started a couple of years earlier while we were in the midst of a strenuous residency programme. Due to long hours and intensity of training, we seldom had free time for meals and sleep, let alone leisure. However, we both shared a burning desire to break free of our confinement, pursue our fantasies and see the world. Only someone who has been through the rigors of medical training would understand why a young doctor is called literally an 'intern' of a hospital during his first year of training, and later a 'resident' during his final years.

During those long years, we colluded and made grandiose plans to travel the world for one year after finishing our training. For unlike most doctors, we did not want to rush immediately into private practice because of the constraints and obligations it entails. Ultimately and true to our dreams, we spent over one year (actually 15 months) travelling within the Pacific Islands, New Zealand, Australia, Southeast Asia, China, Japan, India and the subcontinent, and finally Europe. Our mode of transportation varied from banana boats between the South Pacific islands to wooden canoes paddling down the Sepic river in Papua New Guinea. As part of our adventure, we visited Tibet for four weeks. We flew there by a large four-propeller Russian built plane from the city of Chengdu in China. The plane was carrying primarily Chinese soldiers all dressed in drab blue uniforms of the Mao era. We were the only non-Asians on the flight and nobody spoke English. I could speak a smattering of Mandarin Chinese which I had learned from an English/Chinese dictionary while travelling within China during the preceding two months.

The cabin of the plane was not heated and the noise of the engines deafening. When talking, you could see your breath freeze. Everyone wore thick jackets, hats and gloves. On the positive side, the spectacular view while flying over the Himalayas was breathtaking. We arrived in Tibet in the late spring. During the midday, the temperature would reach between 15 to 20°Celsius, which was comfortable when wearing a light jacket.

However, due to the high altitude (above 15,000 feet) and thin atmosphere, as soon as the sun goes down, the temperature would plummet to the –20's°Celsius or colder. Because of the extremes in temperature, we found Tibet to be an incredibly harsh and unforgiving country. Tibet is also very arid, since most of the rain falls on the other side of the Himalayas in Nepal. Despite their hardships, the people of Tibet are kind, unassuming and friendly. Foreigners are a novelty, and the Tibetans often invite them to their homes and places of congregation.

After we arrived in Lhasa, we rested for several hours. However, being ambitious young explorers, we could not resist visiting the imposing Potala Palace that stood on a high ridge overlooking the city of Lhasa. We climbed the steps slowly, only because the thin atmosphere made us short of breath and our legs feel like lead. Nevertheless, we persevered and after reaching the summit, we took a two-hour tour of the spectacular palace. The palace was enormous and had many chambers and tortuous dark hallways lit by candles. A comprehensive tour of the palace could easily take a couple of days, that is with a guide! Without a guide you are lost.

After our trek to the palace, we returned to the city where we found a Tibetan lodge to stay in. Like all buildings in Lhasa, the lodge was old, cold, dingy and drab. There was no indoor heating or plumbing. There were no luxury hotels in Tibet at that time and only recently were travellers allow to visit. Upon reaching our room, we soon realised the folly of expending too much physical energy immediately after arriving at such a high altitude destination as Tibet.

I was utterly exhausted, dizzy and had a mild headache. However, my friend Jeff became ghastly ill. He complained of a severe, throbbing headache and nausea. He vomited several times, started coughing and felt breathless. Although he was apprehensive and anxious, I convinced him to lie down and stay at complete bed rest. In my backpack, I kept a small medical kit from which I gave him two tablets of paracetamol for his headache and started him on acetazolamide tablets to relieve his cough and breathlessness. I then went down to the hotel desk to enquire about the location of the nearest hospital. Fortunately, it was nearby within walking distance. It was not much of a hospital, and I initially walked right by it.

There seems to be an universal understanding of the English word 'doctor'. For even in an isolated region as Tibet, after inquiring for a doctor I was immediately introduced to one of their physicians. Although his command of English was rudimentary, he understood that I wanted oxygen for a sick visitor suffering from altitude sickness. Apparently, this was a rather common emergency for new arrivals, since he immediately summoned a couple of hospital staff who retrieved a small oxygen cylinder. They knew the way to the lodge. Upon arrival, my friend was relieved to see me, and he was still coughing, breathless and complaining of headache.

We administered the oxygen by a mask which helped considerably in alleviating his symptoms. After half an hour, we transported Jeff back to the hospital, the amenities of which were not any better than at our lodge. Following a couple of days of bed rest, analgesics and acetazolamide, he felt well enough to be discharged from the hospital. During this time, I myself spent most of the time resting and taking acetazolamide tablets to ameliorate the effects of high altitude sickness.

A week after our arrival, we both felt considerably better and able to resume our physical activities and exploration of Tibet.

Jeff and I had learned the hard way of the adverse effects of high altitude sickness. Don't let this happen to you!

If you are planning a trip or hike to a high altitude destination, then be prepared and aware of the dangers!

The easiest way to treat high altitude sickness is to immediately descend to a lower altitude as soon as symptoms begin. This is practical advice when you are on a mountain, but not helpful when on a plateau like Tibet. Medication such as acetazolamide can be taken to help prevent and treat cough and breathlessness. However, more severe symptoms should be treated with oxygen which may not be readily available, except at a hospital.

Above all, after arriving at a high altitude destination, rest and limit your activities. It usually takes a few days to adapt, so catch up on your reading and just relax.

TRAVELLING WITH OTHERS

CHAPTER 16

'When children are doing nothing, they are doing mischief.'
—Henry Fielding (1707–1754), English novelist, dramatist,
quoting 'a wise old gentleman' in *Tom Jones*

Travelling with Children

Their anger and frustration was obvious. The couple were travelling with three young children on a transpacific flight and were struggling to maintain discipline and order. After a couple of hours, the children became bored and were difficult to keep in their seats. Six-year-old Sarah was fighting with her four-year-old brother over an electronic game. The youngest, 20-month-old Bianca was having a tantrum and refused to have her diapers changed. Nearby passengers hastily relocated themselves to other seats.

—A young couple ill-prepared to manage their children during a long flight

TRAVELLING WITH CHILDREN

This young couple's kids are out of control. Better planning of their children's needs and interest should have been done prior to departure. Long distance air travel in itself can be physically demanding, and with the additional care of one or more young children can evolve into a monumental task. As the old saying goes, 'There are two classes of air travel: those who fly first class, and those who fly with children.' Additional considerations when flying with children include: convenient seating arrangements, proper clothing during flights and stopovers, adjusting to changing time zones, food preparations, and an adequate supply of all items necessary in their daily care. It is best to call the airline a couple days before departure concerning particular diets. Many airlines can provide various preparations of baby food, as well as kosher, diabetic, vegetarian or low cholesterol diets.

Be relaxed and arrive at the airport ahead of time. Checking-in and boarding procedures always take longer with children. Rushing will only shorten tempers and there is a tendency to lose, misplace or forget things. Well-organised couples often bring a check-list along. A check-list for babies should include disposable nappies, bibs, baby food (and formulas), bottles, change of clothing, underpants, nappy rash cream, powder, paper tissue and wipes. Phew!

Be self-sufficient! Although most airlines supply baby food, there could be more children on board than scheduled, or there could be a delay between flights. It is also advisable to bring extra disposable diapers for similar reasons.

When it comes to clothing, comfort is the most important consideration. Try to dress with layers of clothing which can be easily removed depending on the ambient temperature of the plane cabin or during stopovers.

In regard to seating, generally the bulkhead areas provide the greatest amount of leg room. However, there is a drawback. The arm-rests of these seats may not be retractable. Therefore, if there happens to be an adjacent empty seat, the child will not be able to lie down. Bassinets can be reserved for infants. Their dimensions range from 60–80 cm long, 30–40 cm wide and about 20–22.5 cm deep.

Toys, books, drawing pads, crayons, colour pencils and games are all important to keep children occupied. Books should be lightweight, full of pictures and fun to read, since you will probably be reading a lot. A small photo album will also captivate children, as well as refresh their memories of relatives soon to be met. For young children, it is a good idea to bring along their favourite teddy bear or doll, since it may provide security and comfort while travelling in unfamiliar surroundings. When children become impossible to manage, try taking a walk within the plane or changing seats. It's amazing what a small change in the environment can accomplish. It is also a good idea to know the names of your flight attendants, which will facilitate assistance.

If you are nursing a child, it is important to drink plenty of fluids to avoid dehydration. Infants can easily adjust to changes in air pressure by either breast or bottle feeding. For older children, bring along lollipops, chewing gum or carton drinks with straws. Infants less than one week old should not fly at high altitude or for long distances, since they may have problems adjusting to changes in barometric pressure.

Motion sickness is a common problem. It can be avoided to a certain extent by sitting children near the wing section or looking out into the horizon. Eating a small, low-fat, starchy meal before and during travel may also be helpful. A mild anti-motion medication such as phenergan (promethazine) can be given before flights. Anti-motion medications are less effective once symptoms have started. They may also have side effects such as drowsiness, blurred vision and occasionally dizziness.

Take-off and landing can be a problem for children with sinus disorders, ear infections, colds or respiratory infections. For these conditions, it is best to seek medical attention prior to departure. Your doctor may prescribe oral decongestants and antihistamines to help alleviate the sinus congestion or blocked nose. Nasal decongestant sprays are particularly helpful if taken just prior to departure or landing.

Many parents administer oral sedatives to their young children during trips. Babies under six months should never be given drugs for sedation. They have their own sleep/awake cycle, and usually during the course of a trip will allow some rest for the parent. For babies between six to 12 months, sedation medication is generally not recommended. These babies usually fall asleep naturally. Older infants and toddlers may be safely given mild oral sedatives. Vallergan and choral hydrate are the sedatives most often used. However, it is best to consult with your physician concerning their indication and dosage. Timing is important, since most children are excited about the trip and are reluctant to go to sleep before their normal bedtime.

After arrival, attempts should be made to adjust meals and sleeping habits as much as possible to the local time zone. If arriving early in the morning, let the children take a short nap (perhaps an hour or two) and then try to keep them awake until their normal bedtime. If arriving late afternoon or evening, try to extend their awake hours until their normal bedtime.

Finally, before any long trip, it is advisable to discuss immunisation and possible health hazards with your doctor. The discussion should include:

- Drink and food precautions
- Malaria drug prophylactics in the tropics
- Soil and water precautions
- Avoiding stray dogs and cats in rabies endemic areas
- The dangers of venomous animals or insects during outdoor recreational activities such as camping or hiking
- Environmental concerns such as sun exposure, altitude sickness and pollution

These topics have all been dealt with earlier in this book and should provide a foundation of knowledge when consulting with your doctor.

If your child has a pre-existing medical condition, it is a good idea to bring along a medical summary as well as an adequate supply of prescription medications. Children should also have their blood group typed. Therefore, transfusions from family members with similar blood types can be given during emergencies. In many developing countries, blood bank screening for AIDS, hepatitis and other blood-transmitted diseases may be inadequate.

TRAVELLING WHEN PREGNANT

Travelling when pregnant is generally safe, unless there is a history of habitual abortions or premature births. Most airlines have limitations concerning travelling during the last month of pregnancy, unless it is essential and authorised by a physician. There is greater fatigue when travelling while pregnant. Therefore, it is a good idea to get plenty of rest prior to departure. Pregnancy is also associated with increased bladder pressure and frequent urination. Therefore, it may be advantageous to be seated at a location allowing for easy access to the toilets.

If you are prone to motion sickness, it would be best to discuss with your obstetrician a safe medication. As with children, all anti-motion medications should be taken ahead of time, since their effectiveness are limited once symptoms have started.

TRAVELLING WITH THE ELDERLY OR PHYSICALLY HANDICAPPED

When travelling with the elderly or physically handicapped, special considerations in regard to transport, diet and health care are necessary.

This group of people may have problems with stability and mobility. Therefore, injuries resulting from falls are always a major concern.

Special transport arrangements may be necessary including comfortable seating with foot-rests, assistance at departure and arrival and wheelchair reservations. Those with respiratory problems may need to prearrange with the airlines oxygen to have on standby in case they become breathless during flight. Special meals can also be prearranged for those passengers restricted to diabetic, or low salt, protein or cholesterol diets.

During long trips, an adequate supply of daily prescribed medications is essential, especially for those suffering from diabetes, cardiac disease or seizure disorders. It is advisable to bring extra medication along in case of a flight delay. Before departure, check with your insurance company to make sure health coverage is up-to-date, and that coverage includes treatment outside the host country. As mentioned earlier, having a medical assistance plan to compliment your health insurance is recommended.

TRAVEL CONCERNS OF THOSE WITH MENTAL HEALTH DISORDERS

Those with unstable mental health disorders or disabled because of senile dementia should never travel alone. People with mild degrees of senility can often compensate for their disability as long as they are surrounded by family and familiar surroundings. However, they quickly become confused and disoriented when travelling in a foreign environment and require constant attention by their companions.

Psychiatric patients with hostile or aggressive tendencies should always be escorted by a health professional and be adequately sedated before and during flight.

TRAVEL TIPS

A Traveller's Ten Medical Commandments

- Keep vaccinations up-to-date and written on the International Vaccination Certificate.
- Take malaria pills wherever necessary.
- Bring along an insect repellent or insecticide and wear a long sleeve shirt at night in areas where malaria is prevalent.
- Disinfect all drinking water when travelling in developing countries. Avoid ice cubes. Avoid fresh vegetables or fruit washed in 'unsafe' water.
- Avoid eating uncooked meat or fish and unpasteurized dairy products in developing countries.
- Don't walk barefoot or swim in tropical regions endemic for soil and water-borne diseases.
- Bring along condoms (also sterile medical supplies when travelling in third world countries).
- Always wear your seat belt and drive carefully.
- Don't forget your first aid bag.
- In case of an accident or illness, contact your medical assistance or insurance company as soon as possible.

APPENDIX

GEOGRAPHICAL DISTRIBUTION OF POTENTIAL HEALTH HAZARDS TO TRAVELLERS

This section is intended to give a broad indication of the health risks to which travellers may be exposed in various areas of the world and which they may not encounter in their usual place of residence. In practice, to identify areas accurately and define the degree of risk likely in each of them is extremely difficult, if not impossible. For example, viral hepatitis A is ubiquitous but the risk of infection varies not only according to area but also according to eating habits; hence, there may be more risk from communal eating in an area of low incidence than from eating in a private home in an area of high incidence. Generalisations may therefore be misleading.

Another factor is that tourism is an important source of income for many countries and to label specific areas as being of high risk for a disease may be misinterpreted. However, this does not absolve national health administrations from their responsibility to provide an accurate picture of the risks from communicable diseases that may be encountered in various parts of their countries. (*This section has been reproduced from *International Travel and Health: Vaccination Requirements and Health Advice*, published by World Health Organisation and the Traveler's Health—Yellow Book [CDC, USA government]).

Africa

North Africa: Algeria, Canary Islands, Egypt, Libya, Madeira Islands , Morocco, Tunisia, Western Sahara

Central Africa: Angola, Cameroon, Central African Republic, Chad, Congo, Democratic Republic of Congo (Zaire), Equatorial Guinea, Gabon, Sudan, Zambia

(to be continued on the next page)

Southern Africa: Botswana, Lesotho, Namibia, South Africa, Swaziland, Zimbabwe

East Africa: Burundi, Comoros, Djibouti, Eritrea, Ethiopia, Kenya, Madagascar, Malawi, Mauritius, Mayotte, Mozambique, Réunion, Rwanda, Seychelles, Somalia, Tanzania, Uganda

West Africa: Benin, Burkina Faso, Cape Verde, Côte d'Ivoire, The Gambia, Ghana, Guinea, Guinea-Bissau, Liberia, Mali, Mauritania, Niger, Nigeria, Saint Helena, São Tomé and Principe, Senegal, Sierra Leone, Togo

North Africa

Access to clean water and sanitary disposal of waste are limited in many areas, so infections related to fecal contamination of food and water remain common and widespread. Vaccine-preventable diseases such as measles, mumps, rubella, and diphtheria persist in the region. More common infections in returned travellers are gastrointestinal: diarrhea (acute and chronic) and occasionally typhoid fever, amebiasis, and brucellosis. Chronic and latent infections in immigrants (and long-term residents) from this region include tuberculosis, schistosomiasis, fascioliasis, hepatitis B and C, intestinal parasites, and echinococcosis.

- **Vector-borne infections**: Many have focal distributions or seasonal patterns. Risk to the usual traveller is low. Vector-borne infections in parts of the region include dengue fever, lymphatic filariasis (especially in the Nile Delta), leishmaniasis (cutaneous and visceral), malaria (risk limited to a few areas), relapsing fever, Rift Valley fever,* sand fly fever, Sindbis virus infection, West Nile fever (especially in Egypt), Crimean-Congo hemorrhagic fever, spotted fever due to Rickettsia conorii, and murine typhus.

- **Food- and water-borne infections**: These infections, which are common in travellers to this region, include dysentery and diarrhea caused by bacteria, viruses, and parasites. Risk for hepatitis A is high throughout the region. Hepatitis E and cholera have caused focal outbreaks, and indigenous wild polio was still present in Egypt in 2005. Other risks include typhoid fever, brucellosis, amebiasis, and fascioliasis (rare in visitors to the area). Intestinal helminths are common in some local populations but rare in short-term travellers.

- **Airborne and person-to-person transmission**: The annual incidence of tuberculosis is estimated to be 50–100/100,000 or lower in most countries in the region. Q fever is widespread in livestock-raising areas.

- **Sexually transmitted and blood-borne infections**: HIV prevalence (in adults 15–49 years) is estimated to be 0.1 per cent, 0.5 per cent or lower. Chancroid is a common cause of genital ulcers. Prevalence of chronic hepatitis B carriage is estimated to be 2 per cent–7 per cent in the region; hepatitis C prevalence exceeds 15 per cent in Egypt.

- **Zoonotic infections**: Rabies is endemic in the region. Sporadic cases of human plague* are reported, and an outbreak occurred in Algeria in 2003. Sporadic cases and outbreaks of anthrax* occur in the region. Avian influenza (H5N1) was found in poultry in 2006; human cases and deaths were reported in Egypt in 2006.

- **Soil- and water-associated infections**: Schistosomiasis is present, especially in the Nile Delta and Valley; it is found focally in other countries. Other risks include leptospirosis.*

- **Other hazards**: Scorpion stings, snake bites, and a high rate of motor-vehicle accidents and violent injuries occur. Screening of blood before transfusion is inadequate in many hospitals.

Southern Africa

Vector-borne infections are common in parts of the region. Access to clean water and sanitary disposal of waste are highly variable but are poor in some areas (especially some rural areas). Vaccine coverage is high in some populations, but vaccine-preventable diseases, such as measles, mumps, rubella, and diphtheria, persist in parts of the region. Polio reappeared in 2006 in Namibia. More common infections in travellers include gastrointestinal infections, African tick-bite fever, and malaria. Infections in immigrants (and long-term residents from the region) include tuberculosis, HIV, schistosomiasis, and intestinal parasites.

- **Vector-borne infections**: Malaria is present in parts of all countries in the region except Lesotho, although the risk is focal or seasonal in many areas. African tick-bite fever (Rickettsia africae) continues to be common in travellers to the region, especially South Africa, Botswana, Swaziland, Lesotho, and Zimbabwe. Other vector-borne infections include tick-borne relapsing fever, Rift Valley fever,* dengue (focal outbreaks but larger areas infested with Aedes aegypti), murine typhus, West Nile fever, and Crimean-Congo hemorrhagic fever.* African trypanosomiasis has been reported from Botswana and Namibia in the past. Tungiasis is reported from South Africa.

- **Food- and water-borne infections**: Risk for hepatitis A is high in parts of the region and outbreaks of hepatitis E have been reported. Risk for dysentery and diarrhea is highly variable within the region. Diarrhea in travellers may be caused by bacteria, viruses, and parasites. Other risks for travellers include typhoid and paratyphoid fever and amebiasis. Cholera is sporadic and epidemic (outbreaks in 2004 in South Africa, Swaziland, and Zimbabwe). Intestinal helminths, although common in some local populations, are rare in short-term travellers.

Excessive sun exposure can lead to sunburn and more serious effects such as accelerated ageing and malignancy. Apply sunscreen when you are outdoors and limit your exposure to the sun.

The traffic pollution in some cities may not be what you are used to. Stay indoors and avoid outdoor physical activities if the pollution index level is in the hazardous range.

Ensure that the seafood you eat is fresh and well cooked, undercooked or improperly stored seafood may give you a nasty case of traveller's diarrhoea.

A food vendor on her way to the floating market in Bangkok.
Trying exotic and tasty delicacies are part of the fun of visiting
foreign countries, nevertheless it pays to be careful about what
you eat and avoid eating raw seafood, meat or vegetables.

Enjoy the outdoors, but keep a lookout for insects and snakes and avoid walking barefooted.

Travelling with young children may seem challenging, but can be surprisingly managable and fun with the appropriate preparation and advice.

- **Airborne and person-to-person transmission**: The estimated incidence rate of tuberculosis is > 300 per 100,000 population in the region.

- **Sexually transmitted and blood-borne infections**: HIV prevalence in antenatal clinics exceeds 25 per cent in many countries in the region; 15 per cent–34 per cent of adults aged 15–49 years are infected. Prevalence of chronic carriage of hepatitis B virus exceeds 8 per cent.

- **Zoonotic infections**: The mongoose is a source of rabies, in addition to domestic dogs and other animals. Plague* is enzootic, and sporadic cases and outbreaks have occurred in Botswana, Namibia, and Zimbabwe since 1990. Anthrax* is hyperendemic in Zimbabwe, with recent outbreaks in animals and also human cases. Sporadic cases of anthrax have been reported elsewhere in the region.

- **Soil- and water-associated infections**: Focal active areas of schistosomiasis persist (caused by Schistosoma mansoni, S. haematobium, and S. mattheei). Cutaneous larva migrans can occur after exposures on beaches. Leptospirosis* has caused outbreaks. Histoplasmosis has caused an outbreak in South Africa.

- **Other hazards**: Motor vehicle accidents and violent injury, as well as snake bites occur. Screening of blood before transfusion is inadequate in many hospitals.

Central, East, and West Africa

Vector-borne infections are common and widespread and pose a major risk to local residents and travellers. Access to clean water and sanitary disposal of waste are limited in many areas, so infections related to fecal contamination of food and water remain common and widespread. Vaccine-preventable diseases such as measles, mumps, rubella, poliomyelitis, and diphtheria persist in the region.

The most common cause of systemic febrile illness in travellers to this region is malaria caused by Plasmodium falciparum. Subacute or chronic infections in immigrants (and long-term residents) from the area include tuberculosis, hepatitis B, HIV, lymphatic filariasis, onchocerciasis, loiasis, schistosomiasis, echinococcosis, leprosy, and intestinal parasites.

- **Vector-borne infections**: Malaria transmission is intense in many parts of the region, including urban areas, where falciparum malaria, much of it resistant to chloroquine, predominates. Sporadic cases and outbreaks of yellow fever have occurred in at least 18 of the countries (especially in West Africa) since 2000; outbreaks were reported in 2005 from Guinea, the Sudan, Côte d'Ivoire, Mali, Senegal, Burkina Faso, and Sierra Leone. All countries in the region are considered to be in the endemic zone, and unvaccinated travellers are at risk for infection. Official reports of yellow fever reflect only a small percentage of all infections. African trypanosomiasis has increased in Africa (it is epidemic in Angola, Democratic Republic of Congo, and the Sudan; and highly endemic in Cameroon, Central African Republic, Chad, Congo, Côte d'Ivoire, Guinea, Mozambique, Uganda, and Tanzania; low levels are found in most of the other countries), and an increase in travellers has been noted since 2000. Most had exposures in Tanzania and Kenya, reflecting common tourist routes. Trypanosoma brucei gambiense is found in focal areas of western and central Africa; T. b. rhodesiense, which causes more acute illness, is found in east Africa. Vector-borne viral infections include dengue fever, Crimean-Congo hemorrhagic fever,* Rift Valley fever,* West Nile fever, chikungunya fever, and O'nyong nyong fever. Lymphatic filariasis is present in many areas; onchocerciasis is widely distributed around river systems, especially in West and Central Africa and as far east as Ethiopia. Another filarial infection, loiasis, is widely distributed in the tropical rain forest, especially in Central and West Africa. Filarial infections are rare in short-term travellers. The rickettsial infections murine typhus, louse-borne typhus, and African tick bite fever (due to Rickettsia africae) occur in the region. African tick-bite fever has been increasingly recognised in travellers to rural areas. Murine typhus is more common in coastal areas. Tungiasis (penetration of the skin by sand fleas) is widespread in tropical Africa, especially West Africa, including Madagascar.

In 2005-2006, massive outbreaks of chikungunya occurred on island countries in the southwest Indian Ocean (Réunion, Mayotte, Mauritius, and Seychelles). Infections were also imported by returning travellers to Europe (160 imported cases in France alone) and the United States.

Tick-borne relapsing fever is widespread in eastern and central Africa and sporadic elsewhere. Epidemics of louse-borne relapsing fever have occurred in the past but pose little risk to usual travellers. Visceral leishmaniasis is endemic in Ethiopia, Kenya, and Sudan (and has caused large epidemics); it is found in the savanna parts of the region. Cutaneous leishmaniasis is also found in the savanna and in Sudan, Ethiopia, and Kenya. Myiasis transmitted by the tumbu fly can affect travellers.

- **Food- and water-borne infections**: Dysentery and diarrhea are common in local populations; diarrhea in travellers may be caused by bacteria, viruses, and parasites (especially Giardia, Cryptosporidium and Entamoeba histolytica). Cholera is sporadic and epidemic. A wave of outbreaks began in West Africa in 2005. Large outbreaks have been reported from southern Sudan and Angola in 2006. Risk of hepatitis A is widespread; sporadic cases and outbreaks of hepatitis E occur. Polio persists in Nigeria (799 confirmed cases in 2005) and was endemic in Niger in 2005; sporadic cases also occurred in Angola, Cameroon, Chad, Eritrea, Ethiopia, Mali, and Somalia in

2005-2006. Other risks to travellers include typhoid (a large outbreak occurred in the Democratic Republic of the Congo in 2004-2005) and paratyphoid fever, amebiasis, and brucellosis. Dracunculiasis cases were reported from nine African countries in 2005, with the highest number of cases in Sudan, Ghana, and Mali, but it is rare in travellers. Intestinal parasites are common in residents in many parts of region but are rare in short-term travellers.

- **Airborne and person-to-person transmission**: The estimated annual incidence rates of tuberculosis (per 100,000) are > 100 in all countries and > 300 in much of the region. Frequent epidemics of serogroup A meningococcal disease occur during the dry season (December through June) in a band of countries from Senegal to Ethiopia. Severe outbreaks have occurred in Burkina Faso, Chad, Mali, Niger, Nigeria, Ethiopia, and the Sudan. Serogroup W135 emerged in Burkina Faso in 2002, causing a large epidemic (13,000 cases). It was the predominant pathogen in 2006 in Kenya, Sudan (W. Darfur camps), and Uganda (Gulu district). Nosocomial and intrafamilial spread of Ebola* occurs in outbreaks (Sudan, Democratic Republic of the Congo, Côte d'Ivoire, and Gabon). Nosocomial spread of Marburg fever virus (an outbreak occurred in Angola in 2005) and Lassa fever virus* has also occurred.

- **Sexually transmitted and blood-borne infections**: The estimated prevalence of HIV in adults (15–49 years) ranges from 1 per cent to 15 per cent in most countries. In most of the region, prevalence of chronic infection with hepatitis B virus exceeds 8 per cent. HTLV-1 is endemic in parts of Central and West Africa. Common causes of genital ulcer disease include chancroid, syphilis, and herpes simplex.

- **Zoonotic infections**: Dogs are the most important source of rabies, which is found throughout the region. A wild rodent is the reservoir host for Lassa fever virus,* which is endemic in West Africa; cases have also been documented in the Central African Republic. Echinococcosis* is widespread in animal breeding areas. Sporadic cases and outbreaks of anthrax* occur in the region (it is hyperendemic in Zambia, Ethiopia, Niger, and Chad and in several countries along the western coast). Monkeypox* is found in West and Central Africa, primarily in remote villages in rain forest areas. Plague* is enzootic, and sporadic cases and outbreaks occur in humans. (Outbreaks have occurred since 2000 in Madagascar, Malawi, Mozambique, Uganda, and Tanzania.) Ituri District (Oriental Province) in the Democratic Republic of Congo reports about 1,000 cases per year and was the site of an outbreak in 2006. Q fever* (airborne spread) is found, especially in West Africa, where livestock breeding is common. Avian influenza (H5N1) was found in poultry in 2006 in Nigeria, Niger, Cameroon, Burkina Faso, Sudan, and Côte d'Ivoire. One human case occurred in Djibouti in 2006.

- **Soil and water-associated infections**: Schistosomiasis due to Schistosoma mansoni and S. haematobium is widespread; S. intercalatum has a more limited distribution (West Africa). Mycobacterium ulcerans (the cause of Buruli ulcer) is most concentrated in West Africa and is increasing in prevalence. Rare cases have occurred in travellers. Leptospirosis* (both sporadic cases and outbreaks) occurs in tropical areas. Other risks include mycetoma and histoplasmosis.

- **Other hazards**: Motor vehicle accidents and other injuries, including violent injury with assault rifles and other weapons, and sexual assaults occur. Snake bites and aflatoxin contamination of grains are common, especially in rural areas. Screening of blood before transfusion is inadequate in many hospitals.

The Americas

North America: Canada, Saint Pierre and Miquelon, United States

The Caribbean: Anguilla, Antigua and Barbuda, Aruba, The Bahamas, Barbados, Bermuda, Cayman Islands, Cuba, Dominica, Dominican Republic, Grenada, Guadaloupe, Haiti, Jamaica Martinique, Montserrat, Netherlands Antilles, Puerto Rico, Saint Kitts and Nevis, Saint Lucia, Saint Martin, Saint Vincent and the Grenadines, Trinidad and Tobago, Turks and Caicos Islands, British Virgin Islands
U.S. Virgin Islands

Mexico and Central America: Belize, Costa Rica, El Salvador, Guatemala, Honduras , Mexico, Nicaragua, Panama

Temperate South America: Argentina, Chile, Easter Island, Falkland Islands, South Georgia, South Sandwich Islands, Uruguay, Bolivia

Tropical South America: Brazil, Colombia, Ecuador, French Guiana, Galápagos Islands, Guyana, Paraguay, Peru, Suriname, Venezuela

---

The Americas
North America

Good sanitation and clean water are available in major urban areas and most rural areas. Many vector-borne infections are found in focal areas and can pose a risk to travellers, especially adventure travellers to rural areas. In temperate areas these infections occur during the summer months. Levels of immunisation are high in most areas. Poliomyelitis has been eradicated.

- **Vector-borne infections**: Lyme disease is endemic in northeastern, north central (upper Midwest), and Pacific coastal areas of North America. West Nile fever was first documented in the United States (New York) in 1999 and has since spread throughout continental U.S. and southern Canada. Other vector-borne infections include Rocky Mountain spotted fever, murine typhus, rickettsialpox, St. Louis encephalitis, La Crosse encephalitis, Eastern equine encephalitis, Colorado tick fever, and relapsing fever. Ehrlichiosis (granulocytic and monocytic) has been reported primarily from the central and eastern thirds of the United States. Sporadic local transmission of dengue has occurred since 1995 in Florida and Texas, and the vector mosquito Aedes aegypti inhabits the southeastern United States. An outbreak of dengue in Hawaii in 2001–2002 was transmitted by Ae. albopictus.

- **Food- and water-borne infections**: Outbreaks of diarrhea caused by enterohemorrhagic Escherichia coli O157:H7 have occurred in many areas and have increased in the past decade. Campylobacter and Salmonella are the most common causes of acute bacterial diarrhea. Giardiasis and cryptosporidiosis occur sporadically and in outbreaks. Outbreaks of diarrhea due to norovirus are increasingly being reported in the United States and Canada.

- **Airborne and person-to-person transmission**: Outbreaks and cases of pertussis have been increasing for more than a decade. The incidence of tuberculosis is low (about 5/100,000 population). Numbers of measles cases have declined in the United States and Canada, and most of these cases are imported or linked to imported cases.

- **Sexually transmitted and blood-borne infections**: The HIV prevalence in adults aged 15–49 years is estimated to be 0.5 per cent – < 1.0 per cent in US, and is 0.1 per cent– < 0.5 per cent in Canada.

- **Zoonotic infections**: Rabies is enzootic in bats, raccoons, foxes, and other wild animals. Human cases are rare. Cases of hantavirus pulmonary syndrome have been widely distributed in North America, with the greatest concentration in the western and southwestern United

States. Tularemia* is found in wide areas of the United States, including Alaska, and Canada, with the greatest number of cases in the central states (Missouri and neighbouring states). Outbreaks have occurred on Martha's Vineyard (Massachusetts). Q fever* cases occur sporadically, especially in persons having contact with livestock in the western part of the region; a number of outbreaks have been documented in the Maritime provinces, eastern Canada. Plague* is enzootic in the western United States, and rare human cases occur, almost 90 per cent from New Mexico, Colorado, Arizona and California, often associated with prairie dogs. Many outbreaks of anthrax in animals were reported in agricultural regions of the US and Canada in 2006; infection in humans is rare.

- **Soil- and water-associated infections**: Coccidioidomycosis is endemic in the southwestern United States and can occur in visitors to the area. Its incidence has increased in Arizona and California in recent years. Histoplasmosis is highly endemic, especially in the Mississippi, Ohio, and St. Lawrence River valleys. Sporadic cases and large outbreaks occur. Hawaii has the highest incidence rate of leptospirosis* in the United States, although sporadic cases and outbreaks have occurred elsewhere, primarily in warmer regions or in summer months. Leptospirosis is often associated with water recreational activities. Non-human schistosomes that cause cercarial dermatitis are widely distributed in freshwater and seawater along the Atlantic, Pacific, and Gulf coasts, and inland lakes.

- **Other hazards**: Violent injury and death related to guns; rates are higher in the United States than in most industrialised countries. Nineteen species of venomous snakes inhabit North America; the highest bite rates are found in southern states and southwestern desert states. Tick paralysis is most often reported from western Canada and the northwestern United States.

Mexico and Central America

Vector-borne infections have focal distributions, and some are seasonal. Access to clean water and sanitary disposal of waste remain limited in many areas, so infections related to fecal contamination of food and water remain common. Levels of vaccine coverage are generally good and improving.

More common infections in travellers to the area include gastrointestinal infections, dengue fever, and myiasis. The risk of malaria is low in most countries; more than half of the cases of malaria in travellers to this region are caused by P. vivax. Chronic or latent infections with late sequelae in immigrants (and long-term residents) include cysticercosis, tuberculosis, Chagas' disease, leishmaniasis, and strongyloidiasis.

- **Vector-borne infections**: Malaria is present in focal areas of all these countries; it remains sensitive to chloroquine in all areas except for parts of Panama. Risk for travellers is low in most areas. Dengue epidemics have affected most of these countries in the past five years. Other vector-borne infections include rickettsial infections (spotted fever and murine typhus) and relapsing fever (tick borne). Foci of active transmission of leishmaniasis (predominantly cutaneous) are present in all countries. West Nile virus has been found in Mexico and may spread in Central America. Localised foci of transmission of Chagas disease exist in rural areas. Risk to the usual traveller is low. Onchocerciasis is endemic in focal areas of Mexico (Oaxaca, Chiapas) and Guatemala; eradication efforts are in progress. Myiasis (primarily botfly) is endemic in Central America.

- **Food- and water-borne infections**: Diarrhea in travellers is common and may be caused by bacteria, viruses, and parasites. Diarrhea caused by enterotoxigenic E. coli predominates, but other bacteria and protozoa (including Giardia, Cryptosporidia, and Entamoeba histolytica) can also cause diarrhea. Risk of hepatitis A is high in many areas; epidemics of hepatitis E have occurred in Mexico. Other infections include brucellosis, typhoid fever, and amebic liver abscess. Nicaragua and Guatemala reported cholera in 2002-2003; however, risk for travellers is low. Gnathostomiasis has increased in Mexico, with many cases being reported from the Acapulco area; infection has been reported in travellers. Intestinal helminth infections are common in some local populations but are rare in visitors to the area. Central nervous system cysticercosis is a common cause of seizures in local residents.

- **Airborne and person-to-person transmission**: The estimated annual incidence rate of tuberculosis per 100,000 population is 25–50 in most of the area, but 50–100 in Guatemala, Nicaragua, and Honduras.

- **Sexually transmitted and blood-borne infections**: The estimated prevalence of HIV in adults is 0.1 per cent – < 1 per cent. Incidence of cervical cancer (due to human papillomavirus) is as high as 33/100,000 women.

- **Zoonotic infections**: Rabies is found throughout the region. Anthrax* is enzootic throughout the region and can infect humans; this disease is most common in El Salvador, Guatemala, Honduras, and Nicaragua. Cases of hantavirus pulmonary syndrome have been reported from Panama.

- **Soil- and water-associated infections**: Outbreaks of leptospirosis have occurred in travellers to the area (including whitewater rafters in Costa Rica and U.S. troops training in Panama); hemorrhagic pulmonary leptospirosis* has occurred in Nicaragua. Sporadic cases and outbreaks of coccidioidomycosis and histoplasmosis have occurred in travellers to the area. Risky activities include disturbing soil and entering caves and abandoned mines. Paracoccidioidomycosis is endemic in parts of

Mexico and Central America. Hookworm infections are common in some local populations but rare in travellers. Cutaneous larva migrans occurs in visitors, especially those visiting beaches.

- **Other hazards**: Scorpion and snake bites and motor vehicle accidents occur. Screening of blood before transfusion is inadequate in many hospitals.

The Caribbean

Access to clean water and levels of sanitation are highly variable in the region. More common infections in travellers include gastrointestinal infections; dengue fever is reported during periods of epidemic activity.

- **Vector-borne infections**: Malaria is endemic in Haiti and is found in focal areas in the Dominican Republic. In 2006, malaria (falciparum) was confirmed in travellers to Great Exuma, Bahamas, and Kingston, Jamaica, areas where malaria transmission typically does not occur. Dengue epidemics have occurred on many of the islands. Most islands are infested with Aedes aegypti, so these places are at risk for introduction of dengue. Lymphatic filariasis has a high prevalence in parts of Haiti; it is endemic in nine of 13 municipalities in the Dominican Republic and Haiti. Spotted fever due to Rickettsia africae has been acquired in Guadeloupe. Transmission of cutaneous leishmaniasis occurs in the Dominican Republic.

- **Food- and waterborne infections**: Risk of diarrheal illness varies greatly by island. Risk of diarrhea and hepatitis A is high, especially on the island of Hispaniola, where an outbreak of typhoid fever occurred in 2003. An outbreak of eosinophilic meningitis caused by Angiostrongylus cantonensis occurred in travellers to Jamaica. Intestinal helminths are common in local populations on some islands but are rare in short-term travellers.

- **Airborne and person-to-person transmission**: The annual incidence of tuberculosis is estimated to exceed 300 per 100,000 population in Haiti and is 50–100 per 100,000 population in the Dominican Republic. The rates are substantially lower on other islands.

- **Sexually transmitted and blood-borne infections**: The prevalence of HIV infection is estimated to be 4.5 per cent in Haiti (1.8 per cent–7 per cent in pregnant women) and greater than 2 per cent in the Dominican Republic. The prevalence of chronic infection with hepatitis B is moderate (2 per cent–7 per cent) in Haiti and Dominican Republic, but < 2 per cent on most of the islands. Seroprevalence of HTLV-I/II is reported to be as high as 5 per cent–14 per cent on some islands.

- **Zoonotic infections**: Anthrax* is hyperendemic in Haiti but has not been reported on most of the other islands.

- **Soil- and water-associated infections**: Cutaneous larva migrans is a risk for travellers with exposures on beaches. Endemic foci of histoplasmosis are found on many islands, and outbreaks have occurred in travellers. Leptospirosis* is common in many areas and poses a risk to travellers engaged in recreational freshwater activities. Foci of schistosomiasis have been active in the past in the Dominican Republic, Puerto Rico, and other islands, but pose little risk to travellers.

- **Other hazards**: Outbreaks of ciguatera poisoning, which results from eating toxin-containing reef fish have occurred on many islands. Injury from motor vehicle accidents (including from motorised scooters) is a risk for travellers. Screening of blood before transfusion is inadequate in hospitals on many islands.

Temperate South America

The overall risk for infections is low for most travellers to the area. Gastrointestinal infections are a risk, especially in rural areas. Chronic and latent infections in immigrants (and long-term residents) include cysticercosis, Chagas' (from remote acquisition), echinococcosis, soil-associated fungal infections (see below), and intestinal helminth infections.

- **Vector-borne infections**: Limited areas of malaria risk are found in Argentina. Dengue outbreaks have occurred in Argentina since 1997, and Aedes aegypti infests the country as far south as Buenos Aires. An outbreak occurred on Easter Island (Chile) in 2002. Other vector-borne infections include bartonellosis (limited to the slopes of the Andes in Chile), tick-borne relapsing fever (reported from northern Argentina and Chile), murine typhus, and spotted fever due to Rickettsia rickettsii (reported from Argentina). Leishmaniasis (both cutaneous and mucocutaneous) is endemic in northern Argentina and may be present in Uruguay. Programs to eradicate American trypanosomiasis (Chagas' disease) have reduced or interrupted active transmission in many areas.

- **Food- and water-borne infections**: Risk of hepatitis A is moderate to high in parts of the region. Diarrhea in travellers is caused by bacteria, viruses, and parasites. Typhoid fever outbreaks have occurred in Chile in the past, and sporadic infections occur in the region. Typhoid fever, amebic abscesses, and brucellosis can be acquired by travellers. Fascioliasis occurs sporadically, but travellers are at low risk.

- **Airborne and person-to-person transmission**: The annual incidence of tuberculosis is estimated to be 25–50 per 100,000 population in most of region, but lower in Chile. Influenza outbreaks peak in May-August.

- **Sexually transmitted and blood-borne infections**: The estimated prevalence of HIV infection in adults is low (0.1 per cent– < 1 per cent). Foci of high endemicity of HTLV-I are found in Argentina and Chile.

- **Zoonotic infections**: Q fever* (airborne spread) is common in areas where livestock are raised; frequent outbreaks have been noted in Uruguay. Rabies is present in the region. Anthrax* is enzootic in Argentina. Sporadic cases of hantavirus pulmonary syndrome (Andes virus; rodent reservoir host) have been reported from Argentina and Chile. Argentine hemorrhagic fever caused by Junin virus (rodent reservoir) is found in an agricultural area of Argentina. Risk to travellers is low.

- **Soil- and water-associated infections**: Histoplasmosis is endemic in Uruguay and parts of Venezuela. Coccidioidomycosis is found in focal areas of Argentina and Chile; paracoccidioidomycosis is highly endemic in Uruguay and in parts of Argentina and sporadic elsewhere. Sporotrichosis is highly endemic in Uruguay and sporadic elsewhere. Hookworm infections are endemic in warm, wet areas but are rare in travellers. Leptospirosis* is a risk in warmer months.

- **Other hazards**: Screening of blood prior to transfusion is inadequate in many hospitals.

Tropical South America

More common infections in travellers include dengue, gastrointestinal infections, and malaria. Chronic or latent infections in immigrants (and long-term residents) include tuberculosis, schistosomiasis, leishmaniasis, Chagas' disease, cysticercosis, and intestinal helminth infections, including strongyloidiasis.

- **Vector-borne infections**: Malaria is widely distributed, but the risk to travellers is low in most areas. Vivax malaria predominates in many areas. Dengue outbreaks have increased in the past decade, and infections occur in travellers. Yellow fever causes sporadic cases and outbreaks. Cases have been reported since 2000 from Bolivia, Brazil, Colombia, Ecuador, Peru, and Venezuela.

Aedes aegypti infests all these countries, including urban areas, placing them at risk for introduction of yellow fever (and dengue). Fatal yellow fever has occurred in unvaccinated travellers. Other vector-borne infections include rickettsial infections (murine typhus and spotted fever due to Rickettsia rickettsii and R. felis), relapsing fever (the tick-borne form is widely distributed; the louse-borne form occurs primarily in the highlands of Bolivia and Peru), and Venezuelan encephalitis. Oropouche fever is a common arboviral infection, especially in the Amazon ba-sin. Leishmaniasis has increased in recent years; foci of transmission of cutaneous leishmaniasis are found throughout the region; visceral leishmaniasis is found primarily in Brazil. American trypanosomiasis (Chagas' disease) has been widespread in poor, rural areas, but transmission has been interrupted or slowed in many areas (e.g., Brazil) through eradication programs. Onchocerciasis is endemic in focal areas of Brazil, Colombia, Ecuador, and Venezuela; eradication efforts are in progress. Bartonellosis is found in the mountain valleys of Peru (largest endemic focus), Ecuador, and southwestern Colombia (at altitudes of 600-2800 meters). Lymphatic filariasis is endemic in Guyana and in focal areas of Brazil and in parts of northeastern South America. Myiasis occasionally occurs in travellers.

- **Food- and waterborne infections**: Gastrointestinal infections in travellers are caused by bacteria, viruses, and parasites. Hepatitis A risk is widespread. Cholera was widespread in South America in the 1990s; only Brazil, Colombia, and Ecuador reported infections in 2005. Typhoid fever, brucellosis, and amebic liver abscesses are occasionally seen in travellers. Fascioliasis is highly endemic in some areas, especially in Bolivia, Ecuador, Peru, and Venezuela, but risk is low for the usual traveller. Paragonimiasis is endemic in Ecuador and Peru and occurs sporadically in other countries; infections are rare in the usual traveller.

- **Airborne and person-to-person transmission**: The annual incidence rate of tuberculosis per 100,000 is estimated to be 100–300 in Peru, Ecuador, Bolivia, and Guyana and 50–100 or less in the rest of the region. Multidrug resistance has been a problem, especially in Peru and Ecuador, where the rate of multidrug resistance is 3 per cent–6 per cent among new cases. Leprosy is highly endemic in some focal areas (e.g., high prevalence in the Amazon and parts of the Andes). Prevalence in Brazil was 46 per 100,000 population in 2004.

- **Sexually transmitted and blood-borne infections**: Prevalence of HIV in adults is estimated to be 0.1 per cent – < 1 per cent in most of the region, but the prevalence is higher in Guyana and Suriname (1 per cent– < 5 per cent). The prevalence of chronic infection with hepatitis B exceeds 8 per cent in Peru, northern Brazil, and southern Colombia and Venezuela and is 2 per cent–7 per cent in the rest of the region. Hepatitis D has caused epidemics of fulminant hepatitis in the Amazon Basin. HTLV-I is found especially in areas adjacent to the Caribbean, including Colombia, Venezuela, Surinam, Guyana, and Brazil.

- **Zoonotic infections**: Rabies is found throughout the region; vampire bats transmit infection in some areas and have been responsible for outbreaks of human rabies in Peru, Venezuela, and Brazil. Hantavirus pulmonary syndrome caused by hantaviruses with rodent reservoirs has been documented in Bolivia, Brazil, and Paraguay; these viruses may be more widely distributed. Other rodent-associated viruses include Machupo virus,* which causes sporadic infections in rural northeastern Bolivia, and Guanarito virus in Venezuela. Plague* has been reported from Bolivia, Brazil, Ecuador, and Peru since 1990 (most cases are from Peru). Echinococcosis* is endemic in cattle-grazing areas of Ecuador and other countries; the risk to travellers is low.

- **Soil- and water-associated infections**: Endemic foci of schistosomiasis (Schistosoma mansoni) are found in Brazil, Venezuela, and Suriname. Buruli ulcer (Mycobacterium ulcerans) is endemic in French Guyana; a few cases have been reported from other countries (e.g., Peru and Suriname). Risk of leptospirosis* is widespread in tropical areas; outbreaks have followed flooding. Histoplasmosis has been reported from all countries in the region, and paracoccidioidomycosis is endemic throughout the area, with the highest transmission in Peru, Ecuador, Colombia, and Brazil. Coccidioidomycosis is more focal in distribution with endemic areas in Brazil, Colombia, Paraguay, and Venezuela.

- **Other hazards**: Venomous snake bites, injury from motor vehicle accidents, and high altitude-related illness in the Andes occur. Screening of blood before transfusion is inadequate in many hospitals.

Asia

South Asia: Afghanistan, Bangladesh, Bhutan, British Indian Ocean Territory, India, Maldives, Nepal, Pakistan, Sri Lanka

East Asia: China, Hong Kong SAR1, Japan, Macau SAR1, Mongolia, North Korea, South Korea, Taiwan
1 Special Administrative Region

Southeast Asia: Brunei, Burma (Myanmar), Cambodia, Indonesia, Laos, Malaysia, Philippines, Singapore, Thailand, Timor-Leste (East Timor), Vietnam

---

Asia
East Asia

Risk of infection is highly variable in the region. Access to clean water and good sanitary facilities are limited in many rural areas, especially in China and Mongolia. Respiratory infections (etiology often undefined) are common in travellers to the region. Chronic and latent infections in immigrants (and long-term residents) include tuberculosis, complications from chronic hepatitis B (and also hepatitis C) infection, schistosomiasis, liver flukes, paragonimiasis (lung flukes), and strongyloidiasis.

- **Vector-borne infections**: Malaria is found in focal areas of China and North and South Korea. Japanese encephalitis (JE) is found in wide areas of China and Japan and focally in Korea. Transmission of malaria and JE is seasonal in many areas. Reported infections in travellers are rare. Other vector-borne infections include dengue, which has caused outbreaks in mainland China, Hong Kong, and Taiwan; spotted fever caused by Rickettsia sibirica (China, Mongolia); murine typhus; Oriental spotted fever caused by R. japonica (Japan); rickettsialpox (Korea); scrub typhus (especially in China, Korea, and Japan); tick-borne encephalitis (in forested regions northeastern China and in South Korea); visceral and cutaneous leishmaniasis (in rural China); lymphatic filariasis (in focal coastal areas of China and South Korea); and Crimean-Congo hemorrhagic fever* (in western China).

- **Food- and water-borne infections**: Risk of diarrhea is highly variable within the region. Diarrhea in travellers may be caused by bacteria, viruses, and parasites. Risk of hepatitis A is high in some areas (excluding Japan), especially in rural areas of China and Mongolia. Outbreaks of hepatitis E have been reported in China. Cases of cholera were reported from China in 2004; most of the cases reported from Japan in 2004 were imported (55 of 66). Sporadic cases of anisakiasis are reported from Korea and Japan. Brucellosis is found, especially in sheep-raising regions of China and Mongolia (annual incidence > 500 per 100,000 population in Mongolia). Paragonimiasis is endemic in China (an estimated 20 million are infected) and still occurs in Korea. Liver flukes (causing clonorchiasis and fascioliasis) are endemic in the region (in 2004 the infected population in China was estimated to be 15 million), but risk to usual traveller is low.

- **Airborne and person-to-person transmission**: The estimated annual incidence of tuberculosis per 100,000 population is 100–300 in China, Mongolia, and North Korea; 25–50 in Japan; and 50–100 in South Korea. High rates of multidrug-resistant tuberculosis are found in parts of China (3 per cent–6 per cent overall in new cases and as high as 10 per cent in some areas). Outbreaks of SARS occurred in mainland China, Hong Kong, and Taiwan in 2003. Measles remains endemic in the region, and infection has occurred in adopted children from China and in travellers to the region. In tropical areas, influenza may occur during all months of the year.

- **Sexually transmitted and blood-borne infections**: The prevalence of HIV in adults is low (0.1 per cent– < 0.5 per cent) in most of the region, but a much higher prevalence is found in focal areas in southern China. Hepatitis B is highly endemic among adults in the region, excluding Japan. Prevalence of chronic infection exceeds 8 per cent in many areas. Prevalence of hepatitis C is 10 per cent or higher in Mongolia; 2.0 per cent–2.9 per cent in mainland China and Taiwan, and slightly lower in the rest of the region. A high prevalence of HTLV-I is found focally in the southern islands of Japan.

- **Zoonotic infections**: Rabies is widespread in China (not Hong Kong) and Mongolia. In 2005, a reported 2545 people died from rabies in China; outbreaks in 2006 have led to mass killings of dogs. Rates of rabies vaccine coverage in pet dogs have been low. Highly pathogenic avian influenza (H5N1) continues to cause outbreaks in domestic and wild bird populations and has caused human cases and deaths in Hong Kong and China. Highly pathogenic H5N1 was also found in bird populations in Japan and South Korea in 2003–2004. Cases of human plague* are reported most years from China and Mongolia. Hantaviruses causing hemorrhagic fever with renal syndrome are a major health threat in China and the Republic of Korea, primarily affecting residents of rural areas in late fall and early winter. Risk to the usual traveller is low. Anthrax* is enzootic in China and Mongolia, and sporadic infection is reported in the rest of the region. Tularemia* occurs in China and Japan and is found especially in northern parts of region. Echinococcosis* is endemic in rural areas of China and Mongolia.

In 2005 a large outbreak of human Streptococcus suis infection caused 215 cases (66 laboratory confirmed) in Sichuan, China. Infection occurred in farmers ex-posed to backyard pigs during slaughter.

- **Soil- and water-associated infections**: Schistosomiasis (Schistosoma japonicum) is present in focal areas in China, especially in the Yangtze River basin. An estimated 60 million people live in at-risk areas. Leptospirosis* is a risk, especially in tropical areas of China and South Korea. Cutaneous larva migrans is common in warm coastal areas. Cases of histoplasmosis have been reported.

- **Other hazards**: Injury from motor vehicle accidents and venomous snake bites occur. Screening of blood before transfusion is inadequate in many hospitals in the region.

Southeast Asia

More common infections in travellers to the area include dengue fever, respiratory infections, and diarrheal infections. Chronic and latent infections in immigrants (and long-term residents) include tuberculosis, late complications of hepatitis B infection, intestinal helminth infections (including strongyloidiasis), and other helminth infections, such as paragonimiasis, opisthorchiasis, and clonorchiasis.

- **Vector-borne infections**: Dengue fever is hyperendemic in the region, and epidemics are common; cases occur in travellers to the region. Malaria is found in focal areas (primarily rural) in all these countries (except Brunei and Singapore), especially in rural areas. Japanese encephalitis is widely distributed in the region and is hyperendemic in some areas; risk is seasonal in some countries. Scrub typhus is a common cause of fever in the region. Other vector-borne infections include murine typhus, chikungunya virus, and relapsing fever. Foci of transmission of lymphatic filariasis are found throughout the area, with the exception of some of the Indonesian islands.

- **Food- and water-borne infections**: Risk of hepatitis A is widespread in the region. Risk of diarrhea caused by bacteria, viruses, and parasites is high in parts of the area. An outbreak of polio (more than 300 virus-confirmed cases) occurred in Indonesia in 2005 after importation of the virus from Nigeria. Campylobacter infections are especially common in Thailand and are often resistant to fluoroquinolones. Amebic liver abscesses, typhoid fever, and brucellosis occur. Isolates of Salmonella causing typhoid fever may be resistant to multiple drugs, including the fluoroquinolones. Cholera epidemics have been common in the past; cases were reported from Cambodia, Malaysia, and the Philippines in 2004. Outbreaks of hepatitis E have been reported from the region (Indonesia and Burma). Cysticercosis is especially common in Indonesia. Gnathostomiasis is endemic in region and especially common in Thailand. Intestinal helminth infections are common in some rural areas; risk to the usual traveller is low. Opisthorchiasis, clonorchiasis, fasciolopsiasis, and paragonimiasis are endemic in parts of the region (especially Laos and Burma).

- **Airborne and person-to-person transmission**: The annual incidence rate of tuberculosis per 100,000 population is estimated to be more than 300 in Cambodia and 100-300 in the rest of the region. Measles transmission persists in the region, although vaccination coverage is improving in some countries. SARS outbreaks occurred in the region (especially in Singapore and Vietnam) in 2003. Influenza infections can occur throughout the year in tropical areas.

- **Sexually transmitted and blood-borne infections**: The prevalence of HIV in adults is 1 per cent– < 5 per cent in Thailand, Burma (Myanmar), and Cambodia and < 1 per cent in the rest of the region. Higher prevalences may be found in specific populations. The prevalence of hepatitis B chronic carriage exceeds 8 per cent in many parts of region. The prevalence of chronic hepatitis C is 1 per cent–2.4 per cent. Chancroid is a common cause of genital ulcer disease.

- **Zoonotic infections**: Rabies is common in the region, and travellers are at risk for exposure to rabid animals, especially dogs. Highly pathogenic avian influenza (H5N1) has been found in poultry populations in most countries of the region. Human cases and deaths have been reported in Thailand, Vietnam, Indonesia, and Cambodia. In 2006, the virus continued to spread in poultry populations in Indonesia. Anthrax* is hyperendemic in Burma; sporadic cases occur in much of the rest of the region. An outbreak of Nipah virus, with a probable reservoir in fruit bats and documented transmission to humans from pigs, occurred in Malaysia (1998–1999) and in Singapore (after contact with pigs imported from Malaysia). Cases of human plague* have been reported since 1990 from Indonesia, Laos, Burma, and Vietnam.

- **Soil- and water-associated infections**: Schistosomiasis caused by S. japonicum is found in the Philippines and Indonesia (Sulawesi [Celebes]); caused by S. mekongi in Cambodia and Laos; and caused by S. malayensis in peninsular Malaysia. Leptospirosis* is common in tropical areas and has been reported in travellers to the area. Melioidosis is a common cause of community-acquired sepsis, especially in rural areas of Thailand; it is also common in Cambodia, Laos, and Vietnam. Cases have increased in 2004 in Singapore. Infection in travellers is rare. Penicilliosis marneffei is found in Southeast Asia and is a common opportunistic infection in HIV-infected patients, especially in Thailand. Rare cases have been reported in travellers to the region. Cutaneous larva migrans is common on warm coastal areas.

- **Other hazards**: Snake bites and motor vehicle accidents occur. Screening of blood before transfusion is inadequate in many hospitals.

South Asia

More common infections in travellers are gastrointestinal infections (including acute bacterial diarrhea and amebic disease), typhoid fever, and malaria. Chronic and latent infections in immigrants (or long-term residents) include tuberculosis, cysticercosis, visceral leishmaniasis, lymphatic filariasis, echinococcosis, and intestinal helminths. Primary varicella may be seen in adults, as childhood infection is less common in tropical areas.

- **Vector-borne infections**: Malaria is widespread in areas at altitudes lower than 2000 m and is found in the Terai and Hill districts of Nepal at altitudes lower than 1200 m. Dengue fever has caused epidemics in all these countries except Nepal. Japanese encephalitis transmission occurs widely in lowland areas of the region (except for Afghanistan). Severe outbreaks occurred in India in 2005. Transmission is seasonal. Focal areas of transmission of visceral leishmaniasis are present in rural India, Pakistan, Nepal, and Bangladesh. Major epidemics of visceral leishmaniasis have occurred in eastern India (especially Assam and Bihar states). Cutaneous leishmaniasis is present in Afghanistan, (where it has infected US troops); India; and Pakistan. Lymphatic filariasis is endemic in large areas of India, Sri Lanka, and Bangladesh. Other vector-borne infections include scrub typhus, murine typhus, epidemic typhus (in remote, cooler areas), relapsing fever, sandfly fever, spotted fever due to R. conorii (especially in India), Kyasanur Forest disease (tick-borne; Karnataka State, India, and Pakistan), and Crimean-Congo hemorrhagic fever* (in Pakistan and Afghanistan). In 2005–2006, an outbreak of chikungunya affected thousands of persons in India.

- **Food- and water-borne infections**: Hepatitis A is widespread, and risk to travellers is high. Large outbreaks of hepatitis E have occurred in Bangladesh, India, Nepal, and Pakistan. Typhoid and paratyphoid fever (increasingly resistant to multiple antimicrobial agents) occur sporadically and in outbreaks and can affect travellers to the region. Amebic infections are common and can cause liver abscesses. Indigenous wild polio was present in in 2005–2006 in India, Pakistan, and Afghanistan; cases from Bangladesh and Nepal were confirmed in 2005–2006. Cyclospora infections have been reported, especially from Nepal. Cholera outbreaks have occurred frequently in the region, especially in Bangladesh and India. Cysticercosis is found, especially in India. Paragonimiasis is endemic in India (Manipur province). Gnathostomiasis has caused sporadic cases and outbreaks.

- **Airborne and person-to-person**: The annual incidence rates of tuberculosis per 100,000 population are estimated to be higher than 300 in Afghanistan and 100–300 in most of the rest of the region. Measles occurs in the region and can be a source of infection for unvaccinated travellers.

- **Sexually transmitted and blood-borne infections**: The prevalence of HIV in adults is less than 1 per cent in most of the region but is rising rapidly in some populations in India (seroprevalence higher than 5 per cent in some antenatal clinics). The prevalence of chronic infection with hepatitis B is 2 per cent–7 per cent in most of the region.

- **Zoonotic infections**: Rabies is common in the region and poses a risk to travellers. Q fever* is widespread. Anthrax* is endemic in much of the region, and cases occur sporadically. Plague* is endemic in India, and outbreaks have occurred. Echinococcosis* is highly endemic in focal rural areas. An outbreak of Nipah virus (encephalitis) occurred in Bangladesh in early 2004, and person-to-person spread may have occurred. Macaques throughout the region are infected with B virus (Herpes). Highly pathogenic avian influenza (H5N1) has been found in poultry populations in India and Pakistan.

- **Soil- and water-associated infections**: Leptospirosis* is common, especially in tropical areas.

- **Other hazards**: There may be a risk for snake bites, injury from motor vehicle accidents, and injury related to ongoing conflicts. Screening of blood before transfusion is inadequate in many hospitals.

Middle East

Bahrain, Cyprus, Iran, Iraq, Israel, Jordan, Kuwait, Lebanon, Oman, Qatar, Saudi Arabia, Syria, Turkey, United Arab Emirates, Yemen

---

Middle East

Common infections in travellers are gastrointestinal infections. Chronic and latent infections in immigrants (and long-term residents) include tuberculosis, echinococcosis, cutaneous leishmaniasis, and brucellosis.

- **Vector-borne infections**: Malaria is present in focal areas of Iran, Iraq, Oman, Saudi Arabia, Syria, Turkey, and Yemen. Epidemic dengue activity occurred in Saudi Arabia and Yemen in 2002. Cutaneous leishmaniasis is widespread and common, especially in countries bordering the Mediterranean. Transmission of visceral leishmaniasis occurs focally in Turkey, Iraq, Saudi Arabia, and Syria. Other vector-borne infections include murine typhus, spotted fever due to R. conorii, tick-borne encephalitis (in Turkey), Crimean-Congo hemorrhagic fever* (in Iran, Iraq, and the Arabian peninsula) (an outbreak occurred in Turkey in 2006), tick-borne relapsing fever, sandfly fever, and West Nile fever. Lymphatic filariasis and onchocerciasis are endemic in focal areas of Yemen.

- **Food- and water-borne infections**: Risk of hepatitis A is high in many parts of the area; typhoid fever occurs sporadically and in outbreaks. Outbreaks of hepatitis E have been reported in Iran and Jordan. An outbreak of polio (478 virus-confirmed cases) occurred in Yemen in 2005 following importation of poliovirus from Nigeria. Cholera was reported from Iran and Iraq in 2004. Brucellosis is widespread and common in parts of the region.

- **Airborne and person-to-person transmission**: Pilgrims to the Hajj (Saudi Arabia) have acquired meningococcal infections caused by serotypes A and W-135, as well as influenza infections. The annual incidence of tuberculosis per 100,000 population is estimated to be 100–300 in Iraq, 50–100 in Yemen and 25–50 in most of the rest of the region. Measles continues to be reported from the region.

- **Sexually transmitted and blood-borne infections**: The prevalence of hepatitis B chronic infection is > 8 per cent in Saudi Arabia and 2 per cent–7 per cent in much of the rest of the region. The prevalence of HIV is estimated to be lower than 0.5 per cent throughout the region.

- **Zoonotic infections**: Anthrax* is enzootic in Turkey, and sporadic cases occur in most of the region except for Oman. Rabies is widespread in the region. Endemic foci of plague* have been identified in the region in the past. Q fever* is common in most countries in the region. Echinococcosis* is endemic in many rural areas.

Outbreaks of oropharyngeal tularemia* have been reported from Turkey. Brucellosis is common in Syria (annual incidence of > 500 per 100,000 population) and has an incidence of 50–500 cases per 100,000 population in most of the rest of the region.

Highly pathogenic H5N1 influenza virus has been found in poultry in Turkey, Iraq, and Israel. Human cases and deaths were confirmed in Iraq and Turkey in 2006.

- **Soil- and water-associated infections**: Schistosomiasis has been found in focal areas in Saudi Arabia, Yemen, Iraq, and Syria.

- **Other hazards**: Motor vehicle accidents, intentional injuries, and injuries related to ongoing conflicts occur. Snake and scorpion bites are an additional hazard. Screening of blood before transfusion is inadequate in many hospitals.

Europe

Western Europe: Andorra, Austria, Azores, Belgium, Denmark, Faroe Islands, Finland, France, Germany, Gibraltar, Greece, Greenland, Holy See, Iceland, Ireland, Italy, Liechtenstein, Luxembourg, Malta, Monaco, Netherlands, Norway, Portugal, San Marino, Spain, Sweden, Switzerland, United Kingdom

Eastern Europe & Northern Asia: Albania, Armenia, Azerbaijan, Belarus, Bosnia and Herzegovina, Bulgaria, Croatia, Czech Republic, Estonia, Georgia, Hungary, Kazakhstan, Kyrgyzstan, Latvia, Lithuania, Macedonia, Moldova, Montenegro, Poland, Romania, Russia, Serbia, Slovakia, Slovenia, Tajikistan, Turkmenistan, Ukraine, Uzbekistan

---

Western Europe

The area is characterised by a low risk for most infectious diseases.

- **Vector-borne infections**: The only malaria cases are 'airport' malaria and imported cases. Lyme disease is found in broad areas of Europe in temperate forested areas. Tick-borne encephalitis is found in Austria, Germany, Finland, Sweden, Switzerland, and Denmark (only on island of Bornholm); a few cases have also been reported from Italy, Norway, and France. Leishmaniasis (cutaneous and visceral) is found, especially in countries bordering the Mediterranean, with the highest numbers of cases from Spain, where it is an important opportunistic infection in HIV-infected persons. Relapsing fever (tick-borne) is found in focal areas in Greece, Italy, Portugal, and Spain; sporadic cases may occur elsewhere in region. Murine typhus is more common in warmer areas, especially Mediterranean port cities. Sandfly fever occurs in warmer months in southern Europe, especially in Italy, Spain, Portugal, and Greece. Small numbers of cases of babesiosis have been reported from the region. A number of countries have reported imported cases of chikungunya fever in 2005–2006.

- **Food- and water-borne infections**: Risk of hepatitis A is low (except for Greenland). Outbreaks of salmonellosis, campylobacteriosis, and other food- and water-borne infections occur, but the risk of diarrhea in travellers is low. Brucellosis is found, especially in southern countries on the Mediterranean. Variant Creutzfeldt-Jacob cases have been reported primarily from the United Kingdom, although a few cases have been reported from other countries. Large outbreaks of trichinosis have occurred; outbreaks in France have been linked to horse meat.

- **Airborne and person-to-person transmission**: Measles transmission has been slowed by vaccination programmes. The annual incidence rate of tuberculosis per 100,000 population is estimated to be 10–50 for most of the region and less than ten in Norway and Sweden.

- **Sexually transmitted and blood-borne infections**: The prevalence of HIV in adults is estimated to be 0.3 per cent in this region.

- **Zoonotic infections**: Large outbreaks of tularemia* have occurred in rural areas in several of these countries, including Sweden, Finland, and Spain. Hantaviruses causing hemorrhagic fever with renal syndrome are widespread. Puumala virus, the cause of mild nephropathia epidemica, is found in Scandinavian and western European countries. Rabies is present in many countries in western Europe; human cases are rare. Echinococcosis* due to Echinococcus granulosus is found, especially in Spain and the Mediterranean countries; areas with alveolar echinococcosis (caused by E. multilocularis) have expanded in recent years, with the largest number of cases found in focal areas of France, Germany, and Switzerland. Q fever* (airborne spread) is a common cause of febrile illness (both sporadic cases and outbreaks), especially in rural areas of Spain, southern France, and other Mediterranean countries.

   Highly pathogenic avian influenza virus H5N1 has been documented in wild birds or other avian species in many of the countries (at least ten by August 2006). No human cases have been documented in this region as of fall 2006.

- **Soil- and water-associated infections**: Legionnaires' disease is sporadic; some outbreaks have involved tourists at resort hotels.

Eastern Europe and Northern Asia

Access to clean water and adequate levels of sanitation are limited in many parts of the region. Vaccine-preventable diseases remain a problem where levels of immunisation are low. The public health infrastructure has deteriorated in areas of conflict; political instability has threatened health in some areas. Common infections in travellers include gastrointestinal infections, respiratory infections, and occasionally vector-borne infections. Chronic and latent infections immigrants (and long-term residents) include tuberculosis (including multidrug-resistant TB) and late sequelae of hepatitis B.

- **Vector-borne infections**: Malaria transmission occurs seasonally in focal rural areas of countries in the southernmost part of the region (Azerbaijan, Georgia, Armenia, Tajikistan, Turkmenistan, and Uzbekistan). Tick-borne encephalitis is widespread, occurring in warmer months in the southern part of the non-tropical forested regions of Europe and Asia. Most intense transmission has been reported in Russia, the Czech Republic, Latvia, Lithuania, Estonia, Hungary, Poland, and Slovenia. Other vector-borne infections include murine typhus, scrub typhus, spotted fever due to Rickettsia sibirica (North Asian spotted fever), rickettsialpox, relapsing fever (more southern parts of region), Crimean-Congo hemorrhagic fever* (in many countries of the region but primarily in persons working with animals or in hospitals), leishmaniasis (cutaneous and visceral, especially in the southern areas of the former Soviet Union), Lyme disease (throughout the former Soviet Union), sandfly fever (in the southern parts of region), West Nile (a large outbreak occurred in Romania in late 1990s), and Japanese encephalitis (transmission occurs in a limited area of far eastern Russia).

- **Food- and water-borne infections**: A high risk of hepatitis A is present in many parts of the region. Sporadic cases of typhoid fever are reported, and outbreaks occur. Outbreaks of hepatitis E have been reported from the southern areas of Russia. Brucellosis is a risk in many areas (annual incidence 50–500 cases per 100,000 population in many parts of the region). Outbreaks of botulism are usually linked to home canned foods. Sporadic cases of fascioliasis occur. A population of 12.5 million is estimated to be at risk for opisthorchiasis in the region (especially Kazakhstan, Russian Federation, Siberia, and Ukraine).

- **Airborne and person-to-person transmission**: The annual incidence rate of tuberculosis per 100,000 population is estimated to be as high as 100–300 in parts of the region. High rates of drug-resistant TB are found in Estonia, Kazakhstan, Latvia, Lithuania, parts of Russia, and Uzbekistan, where rates of drug resistance in newly diagnosed TB patients are as high as 14 per cent. Cases of diphtheria have declined (after the massive outbreak of the 1990s) with improved rates of immunisation. Transmission of measles is declining.

- **Sexually transmitted and blood-borne infections**: The prevalence of HIV in adults is estimated to be 1 per cent–< 5 per cent in many parts of the region. It has increased rapidly in parts of the Russian Federation; seroprevalence in prison populations is 2–4 per cent. The prevalence of hepatitis B is intermediate (2 per cent–7 per cent) or high (more than 8 per cent) in most of the region. The prevalence of hepatitis C is 1 per cent–2.4 per cent in much of the area (2.5 per cent–9.9 per cent in Romania).

- **Zoonotic infections**: Rabies is widespread in the region and is increasing in some countries. Tularemia* is widespread and occurs in focal outbreaks. Wild rodent plague* is broadly distributed in southern areas of the former Soviet Union; human cases are rare. Sporadic cases and occasional outbreaks of anthrax* are reported. Q fever* is found, especially in cattle-raising areas. Hantaviruses causing hemorrhagic fever with renal syndrome are found in many countries in the region; infection is sporadic and epidemic. Echinococcosis* occurs sporadically in the area.

  Highly pathogenic avian influenza virus H5N1 has been documented in wild birds or other avian species in many of the countries (at least ten by fall 2006). Human cases and deaths were reported from Azerbaijan in 2006.

- **Soil- and water-associated infections**: No endemic transmission of cholera was reported in 2004.

- **Other hazards**: Motor vehicle accidents and injuries related to ongoing conflicts and alcohol abuse occur. Nosocomial transmission of infections is a problem in many areas because of inadequate infection control procedures. Screening of blood before transfusion is inadequate in many hospitals.

Australia and the South and Western Pacific Islands

American Samoa, Australia, Christmas Island, Cocos (Keeling) Islands, Cook Islands, Fiji, French Polynesia, Guam, Kiribati, Marshall Islands, Micronesia, Nauru, New Caledonia, New Zealand, Niue, Norfolk Island, Northern Mariana Islands, Palau, Papua New Guinea, Pitcairn Islands, Samoa, Solomon Islands, Tahiti, Tokelau, Tonga, Tuvalu, Vanuatu, Wake Island, Wallis and Futuna

---

Australia and the South and Western Pacific

Risk of infection is highly variable within the region. The risk of food and water-borne infections is low in most of Australia and New Zealand; immunisation coverage is also generally high in those countries. Vector-borne infections and gastrointestinal infections are common in travellers to other islands.

- **Vector-borne infections**: Malaria is transmitted on Papua New Guinea, Vanuatu, and the Solomon Islands. Dengue has caused recurring epidemics on many of the islands and in northern Australia. Japanese encephalitis (JE) is found in Papua New Guinea and the Torres Strait and far northern Australia. JE infections have occurred in the western Pacific islands (e.g., Guam). Lymphatic filariasis is widely distributed on many of the Pacific islands, including American Samoa, Cook Islands, Fiji, French Polynesia, Kiribati, Niue, Samoa, Tonga, Tuvalu, Vanuatu, and Wallis and Futuna. Other vector-borne infections include scrub typhus (in northern Australia and Papua New Guinea and on some of the western and southern islands), murine typhus, spotted fever due to Rickettsia australis (Queen-sland tick typhus), and Murray Valley encephalitis (recurring epidemics are reported, especially in southeastern Australia; rare cases occur in Papua New Guinea). Ross River fever (epidemic polyarthritis) causes sporadic cases and outbreaks in Australia and on a number of the Pacific islands.

- **Food- and water-borne infections**: Risk of hepatitis A is high on many of the Pacific islands. Gastrointestinal infections due to bacteria, viruses, and parasites (including Entamoeba histolytica) have been common on some of the islands, including Papua New Guinea. Typhoid fever is uncommon in Australia; outbreaks have occurred on some of the islands. Cases of eosinophilic meningitis due to Angiostrongylus cantonensis have been reported from many of the islands. Occasional cases of cholera occur in Australia.

- **Airborne and person-to-person transmission**: The annual incidence of tuberculosis per 100,000 population is estimated to be 100–300 for the Pacific islands, and 0–25 for the rest of the region. The influenza transmission season in Australia typically occurs April through September. Periodic outbreaks of measles have occurred on islands with inadequate immunisation coverage.

- **Sexually transmitted and blood-borne infections**: The prevalence of HIV in adults is 0.1 per cent– < 0.5 per cent in most of the region; it is higher (1 per cent– < 5 per cent) in Papua New Guinea and some of the Pacific islands. The prevalence of chronic infection with hepatitis B is 8 per cent on many of the Pacific islands. The prevalence of hepatitis C is 1 per cent–2.4 per cent in most of the area.

- **Zoonotic infections**: Sporadic cases and outbreaks of Q fever* occur in Australia (rarely in New Zealand). Most of the islands are reported to be rabies free, although bat rabies exists in some of these areas. Fatal cases of Hendra virus (closely related to Nipah virus) infection occurred in Australia in 1994. Fruit bats, widely distributed in Australia and the South Pacific, may be the natural host.

- **Soil- and water-associated infections**: Buruli ulcer (caused by Mycobacterium ulcerans) increased in incidence in Australia in the 1990s, with the development of new foci on Phillip Island and in a district southwest of Melbourne. Most cases are in Victoria and Queensland. Cases of melioidosis have been reported from Papua New Guinea, Guam, and Australia; risk may exist on other islands. Leptospirosis is common on some of the islands. Sporadic cases of histoplasmosis have been documented. Hookworm infections and strongyloidiasis are common on some of the Pacific Islands.

- **Other hazards**: High attack rates of ciguatera poisoning from eating large reef-dwelling fish have been reported on some of the islands. Venomous snakes and spiders are a risk in many areas. Screening of blood before transfusion is inadequate in hospitals on many of the islands.

TRAVEL HEALTH INFORMATION SERVICES

- Center for Disease Control and Prevention
  Website: http://www.cdc.gov
  The CDC is one of the major operating components of the United States Department of Health and Human Services. This site provides credible and extensive health and safety information.

- World Health Organization (WHO)
  Website: http://www.who.int/topics/en/
  The WHO is the directing and coordinating authority for health within the United Nations system. Their website provides extensive health information.

- Smartraveller
  Website: http://www.smartraveller.gov.au
  The Australian government's travel advisory and consular assistance service.

- The International Association for Medical Assistance (IAMAT)
  Website: http://www.iamat.org
  Provides travellers with a list of competent doctors around the world who speak either English or French and have had medical training in Europe or in North America. All the doctors have agreed to charge set rates. There is no charge for membership in the organisation, although donations are appreciated. Members get a membership card, a directory of all participating physicians, a traveller clinical record to document your medical needs, a world immunisation chart, a world malaria and schistosomiasis risk chart and an information guide about chagas disease in Central and South America. Visit their website to join or obtain more information.

INTERNATIONAL ASSISTANCE ORGANISATIONS

There are a large number of regional and international medical assistance companies. The following is a partial list of some of the larger companies with extensive networks.

- AXA Assistance: http://www.axa-assistance.co.uk
- Europ Assistance: http://www.europ-assistance.com
- International SOS: http://www.internationalsos.com
- Medex Assistance Corporation: http://www.medexassist.com
- Mondial Assistance: http://www.mondial-assistance.com

CREDIT CARD ASSISTANCE PROGRAMMES

Major credit cards provide a variety of medical and legal services for their clients. In addition, they provide assistance for locating lost baggage, emergency airline ticketing, replacement of credit cards and emergency cash advancement. The best way to find out what assistance services are provided is to directly contact the bank that has issued your credit card. Examples of credit card assistance programmes are:

- Global Assist (American Express)
- Global Customer Assistance Service (Visa International)

GLOSSARY

Anaphylaxis	A severe allergic reaction that may be associated with restriction of the airways, swelling of parts of the body, circulatory collapse and sometimes death.
Antibody	A protein produced by the body to counteract or neutralise a foreign substance (antigen) such as bacteria, virus or toxins.
Anticholinergic	Drugs that interfere with the part of the nervous system involved with the neurotransmitter acetylcholine.
Antihistamine	Drugs that inhibits the effects of histamine in the body. They are often used to treat allergic reactions and allergy related disorders.
Antiseptic	A chemical solution that destroys or inhibits the growth of disease-causing bacteria or other micro-organisms that can be safely applied to skin or mucous membrane wounds.
Antitoxin	A solution of antibodies derived from the serum of animals immunised with specific antigens used to achieve passive immunity or to effect a treatment.
Attenuated-virus vaccine	A vaccine in which there has been a reduction of the disease-producing ability (virulence) by either chemical treatment, heating, drying, or by growing under adverse conditions, or by passing through another organism.

Autonomic nervous system	That part of the nervous system responsible for non-conscious functions of the body such as regular beating of the heart, sweating, intestinal movement , salivation, etc.
Cerebral edema	Swelling of the brain, often the result of injury to the brain.
Chemoprophylaxis	The prevention of a disease by using chemicals or medication.
Cirrhosis	A serious condition in which injury to the liver results in scarring and loss of normal liver cells .
Cutaneous	Relating to the skin.
Deet	N.N., diethylmethylbenzamide, the principal ingredient of effective insect repellents.
Dehydration	Loss or a deficiency of water within the body tisssues.
Dermatophytosis	Any fungus infection involving the skin.
Disinfection	The process of eliminating infective micro-organisms from instruments, the skin or from the surroundings by physical or chemical means.
Diuretic	A drug that increases the amount of urine produced by promoting the loss of salt and fluids from the kidney.
Electrolytes	Any of various ions, such as sodium, potassium or chloride. Cells need them for regulatilng the electric charge and flow of water molecules across the cell membrane.
Endemic	A disease which occurs frequently in a particular region or population.
Enteropathogens	Micro-organisms which are causing disease of the intestinal tract.

Endoscope	An instrument for examining inside the body through a canal or hollow organ such as the stomach, intestines or bladder.
Epidemic	More than the expected number of cases of disease which would occur in a community or region during a given time period.
Frostbite	Damage of the skin or other tissues of the body by freezing. The affected parts, usually the nose, ears, fingers or toes, become pale, blue and numb.
Gastritis	Inflammation of the lining (mucosa) of the stomach.
Glaucoma	A condition in which there is loss of vision as a result of increased pressure within the eye.
Hypothermia	The reduction of body temperature below the normal range.
Hypoxia	The deficiency of oxygen in the body tissues.
Immune globulin	A sterile solution containing antibodies derived from human blood. It is often given by intramuscular injection for passive immunisaition against measles and viral hepatitis A.
Immunisation	The process of inducing or providing immunity articicially by adminstering an immunobiologic. Immunisation can be active or passive.
Immunotherapy	Treatement of or prophylaxis against disease by attempting to produce active or passive immunity.

Inactivated vaccine	A vaccine in which the virulence of an infectious agent has been destroyed usually by heating or chemical treatment (e.g. formaldehyde).
Incubation period	The interval between exposure to an infection and the appearance of the first symptoms.
Intramuscular	Within a muscle.
Isotonic	Having the same concentration of solutes as the blood.
Malignant	Describing a tumor that invades and destroys the tissue in which it originates and can spread to other sites in the body via the bloodstream and lymphatic system. Cancer.
Mammogram	A screening test of the breast using x-rays to detect abnormal growths (or early cancer).
Mucous membrane	Those tissues of the body that secrete a viscid, slippery fluid (mucous) that is usually rich in mucin and helps to protect and moisten.
Parasite	Any living organism that lives within the body.
Passive immunisation	The provision of temporary immunity by the administration of preformed antitoxin or antibodies.
Pasteurize	The treatment of milk by heating to a certain temperature, followed by rapid cooling in order to kill bacteria such as tuberculosis or typhoid.
Peristalsis	A wavelike movement that propels bowel contents down the intestinal tract.

Plasma	The straw colour body fluid that suspends the red blood cells.
Protozoan	A unicellular organism such as malaria or amoeba.
Recommended vaccination	A vaccination not required by International Health Regulations but suggested for travellers visiting or living in certain countries.
Required vaccination	A vaccination the traveller must have for entry into or exit from a country. The traveller must present a validated International Certificate of Vaccination which documents the vaccination(s) received.
Saprophyte	An organism living on dead of decayhing organic matter.
Septicemia	Invasion of the bloodstream by virulent micro-organisms resulting in a serious toxic state associated with fever, chills, prostration and sometimes death. Also called blood poisoning.
Sigmoidoscopy	Examination of the rectum and sigmoid colon with a scope (sigmoidoscope). There are two types of sigmoidoscopes, those that are rigid consisting of a steel or chrome tube, and those that are flexible.
Toxins	A poison of bacterial origin.
Toxoids	A toxin of a pathogenic organism treated so as to destroy its toxicity but leave it capable of inducing the formation of specific antibodies (antitoxin) after injection.
Urethritis	An infection involving the urethra, the canal allowing urine to flow from the bladder out of the body.

Vaccine	A suspension of attentuated live or killed micro-organisms, or fractions thereof administered to induce immunity and thereby prevent infectious disease.
Venom	A poisonous matter normally secreted by some animals (as snakes, scorpions or bees) and transmitted to prey or enemy chiefly by biting of stinging.
Vestibular system	That part of the inner ear and brain involved with maintaining balance.
Virus	A minute particle that is capable of infecting and duplicating within a living cell.

REFERENCES

- 'New Concepts of Cardiopulmonary Resuscitation for the Lay Public'. American Heart Association, 2007.

- *Current Medical Diagnosis and Treatment*. A Lange Medical book, Prentice-Hall International Inc.

- *Current Pediatric Diagnosis and Treatment*. A Lange Medical book, Prentice-Hall International Inc.

- *Harrison's Principles of Internal Medicine*.

- Hotline, AEA, International Newsletters.

- *Manual of Medical Therapeutics*. Washington University, Little, Brown and Company, Boston, Toronto, London.

- *The Medical Letter on Drugs and Therapeutics*. 1000 Main Street, New Rochelle, NY 10801, USA.

- Ministry of Health, Singapore, circular updates.

- *Nelson Textbook of Pediatrics*. WB Saunders Company.

- *Physicians' Desk Reference*. Medical Economics Production Company, Montvale, N.J., USA.

- *Tropical and Geographical Medicine*. Kenneth S Warren and Adel AF Mahmoud. McGraw-Hill Book Company, 1984.

- *Tropical Medicine and Parasitology*. Robert Goldsmith and Donald Heyneman. Prentice-Hall International Inc, 1989.

- *Travel Medicine, A handbook for Practitioners*. Anthony G Turner, Churchill Livingstone (division of Longman Group Limited), 1975.

- 'Guide to Clinical Preventive Services'. U. S. Department of Health & Human Services, 2008.

- WHO, International Travel and Health, Geneva, Switzerland.

- Centers for Disease Control and Prevention Bureau of Epidemiology. Health information for international travel, Atlanta, Georgia.

ABOUT THE AUTHOR

Doctor Paul E. Zakowich is a board certified specialist in Internal Medicine practising in the Republic of Singapore.

He was a chief medical coordinator of AEA, International, an international medical assistance company with an extensive network of medical alarm centres throughout Asia, and in Australia, and the United States. He has helped managed numerous medical evacuations within Southeast Asia.

He writes on a regular basis for the lay press on topics concerning healthcare and travel in the tropics.

He has been a member of the American College of Emergency Medicine, American Medical Association, Singapore Medical Association and Singapore Academy of Medicine.

Dr. Zakowich has resided in Southeast Asia for the past 25 years. His wife, Fiona, is a Singaporean, and they have two daughters.

INDEX

230 **CultureShock!** Travel Safe

Titles in the CultureShock! series:

For more information about any of these titles, please contact any of our Marshall Cavendish offices around the world (listed on page ii) or visit our website at:

www.marshallcavendish.com/genref